Tetralogue

Four people with radically different outlooks on the world meet on a train and start talking about what they believe. Their conversation varies from cool logical reasoning to heated personal confrontation. Each starts off convinced that he or she is right, but then doubts creep in…

Soon their arguments about the reality of witches, scientific proof, faked moon landings, probability, and car salesmen have led them into grappling with questions about truth and falsity, knowledge and belief.

Is truth always relative to a point of view? Is every opinion fallible? Does tolerating an opponent's view actually mean you aren't taking them seriously?

For those new to philosophy, *Tetralogue* is a marvelous way into the subject. For those who are old hands, it neatly poses serious questions about truth and falsity, relativism and dogma.

Meanwhile, back on the train…is Zac heading for a serious slap-down? Can Roxana keep her cool? And is one point of view really right and the other really wrong? That is for the reader to decide.

TETRALOGUE

Timothy Williamson

OXFORD
UNIVERSITY PRESS

OXFORD

UNIVERSITY PRESS

Great Clarendon Street, Oxford, OX2 6DP,
United Kingdom

Oxford University Press is a department of the University of Oxford.
It furthers the University's objective of excellence in research, scholarship,
and education by publishing worldwide. Oxford is a registered trade mark of
Oxford University Press in the UK and in certain other countries

© Timothy Williamson 2015

The moral rights of the author have been asserted

First published 2015
First published in paperback 2017

Impression: 3

Published in the United States of America by Oxford University Press
198 Madison Avenue, New York, NY 10016, United States of America

British Library Cataloguing in Publication Data
Data available

Library of Congress Cataloging in Publication Data
Data available

ISBN 978-0-19-872888-7 (Hbk.)
ISBN 978-0-19-877717-5 (Pbk.)

Printed in Great Britain by
Clays Ltd, Elcograf S.p.A.

CONTENTS

{ PART I }

The Perils of Peacemaking

Sarah: I'll email a complaint the minute I sit down. Nothing will improve unless someone takes the initiative. 'Overcrowding on this train a disgrace...scientific approach needed to predict passenger numbers.' There's a seat. Oh, Bob—what a nice surprise!

Bob: Afternoon, Sarah.

Sarah: It's been ages since we last met. But—your leg! Poor Bob. What happened?

Bob: My garden wall collapsed. I was planting bulbs right beside it at the time. Fell on my leg. The cast will stay on for months.

Sarah: How awful for you—I'm so sorry.

Bob: I'm hardly ever in that bit of my garden. The one time I am, the wall falls down.

Sarah: Yes, that was such bad luck.

Bob: It wasn't a matter of luck.

Sarah: What do you mean?

Bob: Remember that old woman who lives next door to me? Been giving me some nasty looks recently.

Sarah: Maybe you misinterpreted them. She seems quite nice to me. She always contributes when I'm collecting for charity. Anyway, what has she to do with your garden wall?

Bob: More than you might think.

Sarah: What on earth are you getting at?

Bob: She's never really liked me. Convenient for her it fell just when I was there.

Sarah: You're not implying that she pushed it on top of you? I can't imagine for a moment that she would do a thing like that. In any case, she's much too small and frail to push that wall over.

Bob: I didn't mean she *pushed* it over.

Sarah: Then what did you mean?

Bob: I've seen her muttering to herself.

Sarah: We all talk to ourselves sometimes.

Bob: Not ordinary talking to herself. It had a purpose.

Sarah: What was she saying?

Bob: I couldn't hear, but it was nothing good.

Sarah: I'm lost.

Bob: When the wall collapsed, she hurried out into her garden to look. Like checking it had fallen on me. Of course she pretended to be worried. She had to call an ambulance. It would have been too obvious otherwise.

Sarah: There you are. You've just admitted, she was in her house when the wall fell. It must have made quite a noise. Anyone would run out to see what had happened. I'm sure she was as surprised as you were.

Bob: There are ways of making a wall fall over from a distance.

Sarah: Dynamite? That's ridiculous.

Bob: There are words, powerful words.

Sarah: Well, she could tell someone else to push it over, but then you'd have seen this supposed accomplice.

Bob: Words can act in other ways.

Sarah: It almost sounds as though you were talking about a spell!

Bob: That's exactly what I'm talking about.

Sarah: Come on, Bob, this is the twenty-first century. We all know such things don't work. Even if your neighbour *thought* she was casting a spell on your garden wall, which I'm sure she didn't, that obviously had nothing to do with the real cause of its collapse.

Bob: Which was?

Sarah: That wall has been looking pretty dilapidated for some time. The tiles on top were in bad condition, so the rain could easily get in and soak the wall inside. The mortar was missing in lots of places. It was bound to collapse sooner or later.

Bob: Yes, but why did it collapse just when I was planting my bulbs beside it? Explain that.

Sarah: There will be a perfectly natural scientific explanation of why the wall fell just when it did. Through ordinary physical processes of decay, it had simply reached the point of collapse. Unfortunately for you, by sheer coincidence you decided to plant your bulbs at the critical moment.

Bob: 'Coincidence'! That's not much of an explanation.

Sarah: If we knew all the microscopic initial conditions in sufficient detail—

Bob: What do you mean?

Sarah: I mean a description of all the particles and force fields in your wall and brain and their surroundings before the collapse. If we knew all that, together with the laws of physics, we could explain scientifically why the two things happened at the same time. There is no mystery.

Bob: It's easy to say science *could* explain the coincidence. You haven't actually got a scientific explanation, you've just asserted there is one.

Sarah: That's unfair! You don't expect all the scientific resources of the Western world to be concentrated on explaining why your garden wall collapsed, do you? I'm not being dogmatic, there's just no reason to doubt that a scientific explanation could in principle be given.

Bob: You expect me to take that on faith? You don't always know best, you know. I'm actually giving you an explanation. (Mustn't talk too loud.) My neighbour's a witch. She always hated me. Bewitched my wall, cast a spell on it to collapse next time I was right beside it. It was no coincidence. Even if you had your precious scientific explanation with all its atoms and molecules, it would only be technical details. It would give no reason why the two things happened at just the same time. The only explanation that makes real sense of it is witchcraft.

Sarah: You haven't explained *how* your neighbour's muttering some words could possibly make the wall collapse.

Bob: Who knows how witchcraft works? Whatever it does, that old hag's malice explains why the wall collapsed just when I was right beside it. Anyway,

I bet *you* can't explain how deciding in my own mind to plant some bulbs made my legs actually move so I walked out into the garden.

Sarah: It's only a matter of time before scientists can explain things like that. Neuroscience has made enormous progress over the last few years, discovering how the brain and nervous system work.

Bob: So you say, with your faith in modern science. I bet expert witches can *already* explain how spells work. They wouldn't share their knowledge around. Too dangerous. Why should I trust modern science more than witchcraft?

Sarah: Think of all the *evidence* for modern science. It can explain so much. What evidence is there that witchcraft works?

Bob: My garden wall, for a start.

Sarah: No, I mean *proper* evidence, statistically significant results of controlled experiments and other forms of reliable data, which science provides.

Bob: You know how witches were persecuted, or rightly punished, in the past. Lots of them were tortured and burnt. It could happen again, if they made their powers too obvious, doing things that could be proved in court. Do you expect them to let themselves be trapped like that again? Anyway, witchcraft is so unfashionable in scientific circles, how many scientists would risk their academic reputations taking it seriously enough to research on it, testing whether it works?

Sarah: Modern science has put men on the moon. What has witchcraft done remotely comparable to that?

Bob: For all we know, that alleged film of men on the moon was done in a studio on earth. The money saved was spent on the military. Anyway, who says witchcraft hasn't put *women* on the moon? Isn't assuming it hasn't what educated folk call 'begging the question'?

Sarah: I can't believe I'm having this conversation. Do you seriously deny that scientific journals are full of evidence for modern scientific theories? Isn't all of that evidence against witchcraft?

Bob: How do we know how much of that so-called evidence is genuine? There have been lots of scandals recently about scientists faking their results. For all we know, the ones who get caught are only the tip of the iceberg.

Sarah: Well, if you prefer, look at all the successful technology around you. You're sitting on a train, and I notice you have a laptop and a mobile phone. Think of all the science that went into them. You're not telling me *they* work by witchcraft, are you?

Bob: Lots of modern science and technology is fine in its own way. I went to hospital by ambulance, not broom, thank goodness. None of that means modern science can explain everything.

Sarah: If all that modern science is fine in its own way, isn't the evidence for it evidence against witchcraft, just as I said?

Bob: I don't see why. You seem to think modern science implies witchcraft doesn't work. Why are you so sure? As far as I know, those scientific theories of yours don't say anything directly about witches, for or against. For that matter, they don't say anything directly about politicians either, for or against. That doesn't mean modern science implies political propaganda doesn't work. Why is it any different for witchcraft?

Sarah: But isn't witchcraft supposed to involve forces unknown to modern science that would interfere with its predictions?

Bob: They may be unknown to modern science, but does modern science claim to know everything? Witchcraft may even work in accordance with the laws of science, using them for its own ends. Perhaps witchcraft helps make science's predictions come true.

Sarah: In principle maybe that can't be ruled out yet, but in practice, if witchcraft *really* worked, shouldn't we have better evidence of it by now? For instance, wouldn't some witches give in to the temptation to make a fortune by successfully performing witchcraft on television? Think of the viewing figures when it is announced that a famous personality will be turned into a frog on a live broadcast tonight!

Bob: Even if a witch did that, most people would think it was just some sort of trick. To be honest, I'm not sure witchcraft would work in such conditions. The magic may protect itself from public exposure. It's not meant for everyone.

Sarah: How convenient. You keep explaining away the shortage of evidence for witchcraft. Let's put it this way. There is massive evidence in favour of modern science. There is no serious evidence in favour of witchcraft. It's known in most historical cases of alleged witchcraft that the accused were poor, innocent old women denounced by neighbours who felt guilty about not giving them charity, or else they were folk healers turned on by clients whose children they couldn't cure, or other such people. You can't expect me to believe that all those confessions extracted under sadistic torture in the sixteenth and seventeenth centuries were true. Isn't the hypothesis that witchcraft is just a myth by far the simplest explanation of the phenomena?

Bob: Simplicity isn't truth. You're right, lots of so-called witches are not real witches. Maybe most of them. Some of those randy middle-class women who like dancing around naked at midnight are definitely frauds. But that doesn't mean there are no genuine witches. People who say they're wise are not wise, but still: some people really are wise. Too wise to say they're wise. Too much has happened to me and other people I know to explain except by witchcraft. When I look at all that evidence, it's pretty obvious, there are real witches. That old woman next door is one. Just look at my leg.

Sarah: Is it only witchcraft, or do you believe in all sorts of other superstitions as well?

Bob: 'Superstition'! I know about witchcraft from my own personal experiences of it, not just from what other people tell me or I read in books. About things I haven't experienced, I try to be open-minded.

Sarah: 'Open-minded'! You just interpret your experiences in terms of your preconceived ideas. You twist the story of your garden wall to suit your desire for a scapegoat to blame your misfortune on.

Bob: 'Twist'! You didn't see the look on that old woman's face. I did. She's the twister.

Sarah: It's pointless arguing with you. Nothing will shake your faith in witchcraft!

Bob: Will anything shake *your* faith in modern science?

Zac: Excuse me, folks, for butting in: sitting here, I couldn't help overhearing your conversation. You both seem to be getting quite upset. Perhaps I can help. If I may say so, each of you is taking the superior attitude 'I'm right and you're wrong' toward the other.

Sarah: But I *am* right and he *is* wrong.

Bob: No. *I'm* right and *she's* wrong.

Zac: There, you see: deadlock. My guess is, it's becoming obvious to both of you that neither of you can definitively *prove* the other wrong.

Sarah: Maybe not right here and now on this train, but just wait and see how science develops—people who try to put limits to what it can achieve usually end up with egg on their face.

Bob: Just *you* wait and see what it's like to be the victim of a spell. People who try to put limits to what witchcraft can do end up with much worse than egg on their face.

Zac: But isn't each of you quite right, from your own point of view? What you—

Sarah: Sarah.

Zac: Pleased to meet you, Sarah. I'm Zac, by the way. What Sarah is saying makes perfect sense from the point of view of modern science. And what you—

Bob: Bob.

Zac: Pleased to meet you, Bob. What Bob is saying makes perfect sense from the point of view of traditional witchcraft. Modern science and traditional witchcraft are different points of view, but each of them is valid on its own terms. They are equally intelligible.

Sarah: They may be equally intelligible, but they aren't equally *true*.

Zac: 'True': that's a very dangerous word, Sarah. When you are enjoying the view of the lovely countryside through this window, do you insist that you are seeing right, and people looking through the windows on the other side of the train are seeing wrong?

Sarah: Of course not, but it's not a fair comparison.

Zac: Why not, Sarah?

Sarah: We see different things through the windows because we are looking in different directions. But modern science and traditional witchcraft ideas are looking at the *same* world and say incompatible things about it, for instance about what caused Bob's wall to collapse. If one side is right, the other is wrong.

Zac: Sarah, it's you who make them incompatible by insisting that someone must be right and someone must be wrong. That sort of judgemental talk comes from the idea that we can adopt the point of view of a God, standing in judgement over everyone else. But we are all just human beings. We can't make definitive judgements of right and wrong like that about each other.

Sarah: But aren't you, Zac, saying that Bob and I were both *wrong* to assume there are right and wrong answers on modern science versus witchcraft, and that you are *right* to say there are no such right and wrong answers? In fact, aren't you contradicting yourself?

Zac: I just said that each of you is right from your own point of view, and that it isn't helpful for either of you to set yourself up in judgement over the other.

Sarah: Aren't you setting yourself up in judgement over both of us?

Zac: I'm not judging anyone, Sarah. I'm just trying to help.

Sarah: Well, I'm trying to help Bob by explaining to him that he doesn't have to worry about spells cast by his next door neighbour. We can all get more help from modern science than we can from witchcraft.

Bob: How's modern science going to help me combat a spell?

Sarah: By showing you there's no spell to combat.

Zac: Sarah, don't you see, Bob *is* getting help from taking the witchcraft point of view? This shocking, painful, troublesome thing has happened to him: out of the blue, a collapsing wall has crushed his leg. Misfortune is *especially* hard to bear when it seems to make no sense. By taking the witchcraft point of view, Bob has managed to make sense of his misfortune. It has a meaning for him, and—if I may so, Bob—you seem to be bearing up pretty well. If Bob feels his misfortune wouldn't make sense for him if he took the modern scientific point of view—it would just be a random, pointless accident—who are you and I, Sarah, to object if he takes the traditional witchcraft point of view? Right now, it probably gives him more help than modern science would.

Sarah: It's a good thing our society as a whole doesn't take the point of view of traditional belief in witchcraft. If it did, Bob's denunciation could get that innocent old woman burnt at the stake.

Bob: Innocent, my foot!

Sarah: Witch trials are the kind of 'help' our society can do without. Modern science has freed us from that sort of superstition and enabled us to approach questions more rationally, on the basis of proper evidence. We know better than the witch-burners did.

Zac: I don't want to burn any witches, Sarah. The witch-burners were being judgemental in just the way I was critiquing. But historians working on the witch trials have to understand the point of view of the witch-burners, otherwise they can't make sense of what happened. The witch-burners didn't see themselves as being in the grip of irrational superstition.

Sarah: Obviously not, but they still *were* in the grip of irrational superstition.

Zac: Have you ever studied seventeenth-century theories of witchcraft, Sarah?

Sarah: I don't need to.

Zac: They had their own sophisticated logic. What right have you, Sarah, to insist that everyone else must take your point of view, especially when you haven't even bothered to find out what their alternative point of view actually is?

Sarah: It isn't just *my* point of view, it's the point of view of modern science. It's the best point of view available. There is such a thing as progress. Courts of law today accept evidence from DNA tests. Do you think they should accept evidence from ducking-stools and suchlike traditional tests of witchcraft?

Zac: Well, Sarah, that isn't my own point of view.

Sarah: What's the difference, from your point of view? Why should the courts accept evidence based on modern scientific theories but not evidence based on traditional ideas about witchcraft?

Zac: In our society, Sarah, modern scientific theories are much more widely respected than traditional ideas about witchcraft.

Sarah: I didn't ask you why some kinds of evidence and not others *are* accepted by the courts, I asked you why they *should be* accepted.

Zac: Sarah, in any society, public decision-making bodies like law courts need general credibility in order to play their role properly. They have to be regarded as legitimate by the people. If their decisions weren't treated as final, it would lead to chaos. The courts lose that credibility if they accept evidence based on theories with low social prestige, or reject evidence based on theories with high prestige.

Sarah: So if traditional witchcraft beliefs regain high prestige, the courts should accept evidence based on them?

Zac: Right now, we don't belong to a society where witchcraft beliefs have high prestige. The legal procedures of such a society are for *its* members to decide, not for us. For better or worse, traditional beliefs about witches happen to have low prestige in our society at present.

Bob: That doesn't mean they're false.

Zac: I agree, Bob.

Bob: Law courts might make better decisions if they started taking witchcraft seriously.

Zac: What do you mean by 'better', Bob?

Bob: Convicting more of the guilty, fewer of the innocent.

Zac: But who is to decide who is guilty and who is innocent, if not a publicly accredited court of law?

Bob: Can't a court get its verdict wrong?

Zac: Well, some verdicts are reversed on appeal.

Bob: I don't just mean that. Imagine the woman next door being prosecuted today for inflicting grievous bodily harm on me. No way would she be convicted. I couldn't appeal against the verdict of innocent. But we all know, she'll never even be prosecuted, let alone convicted. None of that means she isn't guilty.

Zac: Who is to be the judge of whether she inflicted grievous bodily harm on you, Bob? You can't expect to be judge and jury in your own case, any more than your neighbour can.

Bob: I don't want to be a judge. I just think the courts could do a better job by not being so narrow-minded and legalistic about what sort of evidence they accept.

Sarah: Aren't courts legalistic by definition?

Bob: You know what I mean. In times past, courts didn't accept DNA evidence. *You* must think it's better now they do, Sarah.

Sarah: Yes, of course.

Bob: It would be better still if they accepted evidence based on traditional knowledge about witches. But I see they won't until more people with power and influence—not just ordinary people like me—start respecting that knowledge once more. What do you think it would take, Zac, for that to happen, for our society to respect the reality of witchcraft like it once did?

Zac: Well, Bob, I suppose, if those beliefs were taught to children in schools, and studied in leading universities, then in the long run they would be far more widely accepted. Obviously, they would have to be taught the way modern scientific theories are taught, not just as quaint beliefs people long ago once held, and some people in so-called 'primitive' societies still hold.

Bob: That would be only fair. Then people could make up their own minds about it, without being frightened off by ignorant stories.

Sarah: If I had *your* views, Bob, I would write a letter to the newspapers demanding that all children be taught in school about witchcraft, and that it be studied in universities, just as modern science is. Of course, *I* won't sign. I thoroughly disapprove of the proposal.

Bob: That's an idea, Sarah. Will you sign, Zac?

Zac: Umm, I don't think so, thanks.

Bob: Why not?

Zac: Personally, I don't think in terms of witchcraft. I don't find that vocabulary useful.

Sarah: The letter I'm imagining on Bob's behalf wouldn't call for the teaching of modern scientific theories in school to be abolished, or for them not to be studied in universities. It would only demand equal time and funding for the teaching and study of traditional witchcraft beliefs *and* modern scientific theories. What's objectionable about that from your point of view, Zac?

Zac: There isn't time for *everything* to be taught in school. Choices have to be made. Since modern scientific theories are more central to our society than traditional witchcraft beliefs, isn't it reasonable for our educational system to give them priority?

Bob: From what you were saying before, if modern science is more fashionable in our society today than witchcraft, that's down to the difference in how schools treat them. Aren't you really saying we should teach our children whatever we were taught? Isn't that a vicious circle? Anyway, how do you know witchcraft *isn't* central to our society, right now? As I was trying to explain to Sarah, lots of things happen that can only be properly explained by witchcraft. If people in our society are suffering injury, illness, misfortune, even death, by witchcraft, doesn't that make it important enough to deserve being taught in schools and colleges?

Zac: Bob, do you sincerely expect such a change in the educational system?

Bob: No time soon, of course. In fifty years, perhaps. If it would be a good change, why shouldn't I campaign for it?

Zac: Bob, would you define 'good change' for me?

Bob: Define it yourself. Would you have used delaying tactics like that against campaigners for the abolition of slavery? When they said it would be a good change, would you have told them to define 'good change'? Put it your way: if teaching all children about witchcraft would be a good change 'from my point of view', why shouldn't I campaign for it?

Zac: I'm not stopping you, Bob.

Bob: But will you help me?

Zac: Not that way, Bob.

Bob: Why not?

Zac: I've already told you, Bob. It wouldn't be a good change from *my* point of view.

Bob: When you first interrupted Sarah's argument with me, I thought you wanted to defend me against her intellectual snobbery.

Sarah: That's not fair!

Bob: All right, call it superior education, if you want. I didn't think you, Zac, actually *believed* in witchcraft, I just thought you were open-minded about it. Now I realize you're just as prejudiced against it as Sarah is.

Sarah: That isn't fair either! My disbelief is based on evidence and reason, not prejudice.

Bob: Put it how you like, you don't take witchcraft seriously. My point is: at first I thought Zac took it more seriously than you do, now I realize he doesn't.

Zac: I take witchcraft very seriously as a point of view, Bob, just as I take modern science very seriously as a point of view.

Bob: You just mean you know people like me sincerely *believe* in witchcraft, and so did many more people in times past and still in some foreign countries.

Zac: Just as I also know that people like Sarah sincerely believe in modern science, Bob, and that such *beliefs* have become influential in most societies.

Bob: There's something more in your attitude to modern science than in your attitude to witchcraft.

Zac: How do you mean, Bob?

Bob: Imagine you, Zac, start feeling terribly ill. I hope you won't, but you never can tell. You wait a couple of days, but you feel no better. You go to a doctor. He passes you on to a specialist, who orders various fancy tests, based on modern medical science, looks at the results, decides what's wrong with you, and tells you what drugs you must take and what treatments you must have, also based on modern medical science, to feel better, even to save your life. You'll follow the doctor's orders, won't you? You won't go to a wise woman who knows about witchcraft and follow *her* advice instead.

Zac: I'm a typical Western white male, I admit. People with my point of view trust modern scientific medicine more than they trust traditional witchcraft-based remedies. But I acknowledge, your point of view is different, and I respect it equally.

Bob: What use is equal respect if it doesn't imply equal trust?

Sarah: Hang on a minute, Bob. Your leg was set in plaster in a regular hospital, wasn't it? You didn't go to a traditional wise woman who knows about witchcraft for that, did you? The doctors at the hospital are trained in modern medical science, not in witchcraft. Are you sure that you yourself have the courage of your supposed convictions?

Bob: What could I do? It's true, I was treated in the local hospital. Its reputation isn't too bad. It was only in the ambulance on the way there I thought about what had happened. It suddenly came to me, it was all the fault of that old hag next door. By then it was too late. I was worried, I can tell you, specially as it was her who called the ambulance. I wondered who was really driving it, and where it was really taking me. With my leg as it was and the ambulance going so fast, there was no hope of escape. But I don't think she wants me dead. That would bring the police round, snooping and asking awkward questions. Their prying wouldn't suit her. Anyway, as soon as I was discharged from the hospital, I hobbled over to a wise woman I know. She rubbed special herbs on the cast to protect it from any spells the hag tried to put on it. The herbs have worked brilliantly. She also gave me a special ointment to rub on other parts of my body which were hurting. I used it instead of the painkillers they gave me in hospital and soon felt much better. That wise woman is a wonder. For years I had back pains the doctors could do nothing about. She gave me a little pouch to wear round my neck. The next morning the back pains had gone. They've never come back.

Sarah: The placebo effect.

Bob: Whatever it is, it works. I often consult her now about my problems. She's such a help. She told me the hospital's treatment of my leg did no harm because the spell was on the wall, not on my leg. Last year she told me to stop watching TV because it was causing my headaches. I got rid of my TV set and now I hardly ever have headaches.

Sarah: Do you pay her for her services?

Bob: She never asks for money. I always bring her a small present. That's only polite. I gave her some money when she cured my back pains. She didn't want to accept it, but I insisted.

Sarah: I apologize, Bob, for doubting your sincerity. You really do believe in that stuff. You put your money where your mouth is. And you must admit, Zac, any respect you may have for traditional folk medicine doesn't involve as much trust as your respect for modern scientific medicine.

Zac: I'm sure some of those traditional folk remedies are highly effective, Sarah.

Sarah: Saying so is a long way from actually consulting a traditional wise woman, following her advice instead of doing what the doctors say, and paying her for it.

Zac: Sarah, I never said traditional folk medicine is as effective *for me* as modern scientific medicine. I don't pretend to tell other people what sort of medicine they should use. I respect every form of medicine as part of a genuine way of life.

Bob: Have you ever been to a wise woman?

Zac: There's a woman doctor I sometimes consult about my diabetes, Bob. I regard her as pretty wise.

Bob: You know that's not what I meant. Have you ever been to a woman who knows about witchcraft and how to protect you from it?

Zac: No, I haven't, Bob.

Bob: How do you know your so-called diabetes isn't caused by witchcraft? Your doctors haven't cured it, have they?

Zac: No, Bob, of course not, one couldn't expect that. But they have been invaluable in helping me manage it.

Bob: If it's caused by witchcraft, my wise woman may be able to do much better than that. Look, I have her number here on my phone. I'll call her for you here and now, explain the situation, and hand you over to make an appointment with her.

Zac: No, thank you, it's very kind of you, Bob, but I don't think I will.

Bob: Why not? You could at least give her a try. If you don't like her advice, you can just ignore it—though you'd be making a big mistake. You have a very serious illness. It makes your life difficult and dangerous. Your doctors can't cure it. Why don't you even want to find out about an alternative approach, which might remove your affliction? How do you know it wouldn't work? You won't have to pay her if you don't want to.

Zac: It's not the cost that worries me, Bob. From my point of view, it just isn't a promising suggestion.

Bob: As far as I can see, you only pay lip service to the idea of respecting my point of view. You don't take it seriously enough to lift a finger to find out whether it's better than yours, even when your life may depend on it. You don't really think there's the slightest chance witchcraft caused your affliction. If you did, you'd act quite differently. I prefer Sarah's way of rejecting my beliefs. She doesn't even pretend to respect them. She's quite open in her disagreement. She argues with what I say directly, one person against another. At least she takes my point of view seriously enough to treat it as a competitor with hers, even though it's one she despises.

Sarah: That's a little harsh!

Bob: You know it's what you think. Anyway, I prefer Sarah's attitude. She treats me seriously enough to argue against me. Your attitude, Zac, is to patronize me by telling me how much you respect my point of view while actually not taking it seriously enough to bother arguing against it. For you it's not a competitor you despise, it's not even in the race.

Zac: Why does there have to be a race, Bob? Why can't different points of view co-operate with each other instead of competing?

Sarah: Isn't there a competition to be *your* point of view? You can't simultaneously take the point of view of modern scientific theories and that of traditional witchcraft beliefs. If the advice of a traditional wise woman conflicts with that of your doctors, you can't follow both. When it comes down to it, you accept your own point of view and you reject Bob's.

Zac: That doesn't mean my point of view is *better* than anyone else's, Sarah.

Sarah: Nobody is saying your point of view is better than anyone else's, Zac.

Zac: I don't despise your point of view, Sarah.

Sarah: I'm glad to hear it.

Zac: And I don't despise yours either, Bob.

Bob: That's what you say.

Sarah: Zac, whenever questions arise about whose point of view to prefer, you fall back on the idea that different points of view are separate but equal. That way you protect your own point of view from serious criticism and competition, where each side risks coming off worse than the other. You protect yourself from learning better. For instance, you seem pretty pleased with your point of view on points of view. That point of view is what some people would call 'relativism', I believe.

Zac: Yes, Sarah, you can call my point of view 'relativism' if you like. It's the point of view of many people who have reflected on the harm done by the opposite attitude to points of view, call it 'absolutism' if you like, which insists on classifying points of view as 'right' or 'wrong'. Absolutism has led to the death of millions of people in the name of God or progress.

Sarah: When you say that, aren't you implicitly classifying relativism as 'right' and absolutism as 'wrong'?

Zac: No, Sarah, you tried to trip me into that old trap before. I would only classify relativism as 'my own present point of view' and absolutism as 'someone else's present point of view'.

Sarah: But weren't you trying to give Bob and me a reason to *prefer* relativism over absolutism? Don't you regard relativism as in some way a *better* point of view than absolutism?

Zac: Not in the sense of one being right and the other wrong, Sarah, no.

Sarah: But in some other sense?

Zac: As I said, Sarah, millions of people have been massacred in the name of absolutist points of view. Has anyone ever been massacred in the name of relativism?

Sarah: You seem to be suggesting that relativism is preferable to absolutism because adopting it does less harm. You are judging points of view in terms of their good or bad effects.

Bob: What if science ends up destroying the whole human race by pollution or weapons of mass destruction, which may well happen? Then, by Zac's standard, belief in witchcraft is much better than belief in modern science—on any reckoning it never did anything like so much harm.

Sarah: Yes, even though there never were any witches! You can't blame science for the evil uses military and political leaders make of it. And you can't stop scientific progress. Surely Bob's point about the possible end of the human species shows that the truth or falsity of a belief is a different question from the good or bad effects of believing it.

Zac: Sarah, I'm only discussing the *effects* of taking one point of view rather than another. It's the absolutist who uses dogmatic words like 'truth' and 'falsity'.

Sarah: But how do you decide whether the effects *are* good or bad? Are you an absolutist or a relativist about that?

Zac: I'm not an absolutist about anything, Sarah. Effects can be good for one person, bad for another.

Sarah: Massacres may be good from the point of view of those who commit them. If Hitler in his bunker in late April 1945 could have pressed a button to wipe out the whole human race, he would probably have done so. From *his* point of view that outcome would have been better than an Allied victory. Aren't you assuming that a peaceful life is better than a violent death?

Zac: It is better from my point of view, Sarah. Isn't it better from yours?

Bob: It is from mine.

Sarah: And from mine too, of course. But what has that to do with relativism? Couldn't someone be a relativist and still prefer violent death to peaceful life?

Zac: Hitler wasn't a relativist, Sarah.

Sarah: I'm not saying he was. I'm just saying, if relativism is compatible with preferring peaceful civilization to the extinction of humanity, it is equally compatible with preferring the extinction of humanity to peaceful civilization. It implies nothing about which is better.

Zac: Relativists don't want to impose their point of view on other people, Sarah. Killing people is the ultimate way of imposing your point of view on them. Leaving them in peace isn't imposing anything.

Sarah: You seem to be saying that relativism implies that tolerance is better than intolerance. I don't see how.

Zac: If I can't say my point of view is right and yours is wrong, Sarah, what right have I to impose my point of view on you?

Sarah: Do you mean what absolute right, or what right from your own point of view?

Zac: I mean what right from my point of view as a relativist, Sarah.

Sarah: Well, maybe *you* have no right from *your* personal point of view, but from the point of view of some *other* relativist, a less amiable one, why shouldn't he have the right to impose his point of view on everyone else?

Zac: Relativism doesn't imply that, Sarah.

Sarah: I'm not saying relativism does imply that a malevolent relativist has the right to impose his point of view on others. My point is, it *doesn't* imply that he has *no* right to impose his point of view. It's just neutral. What we do or don't have a right to do is a matter of morality. Surely it's against the spirit of relativism to say what the 'right' moral code is. If relativism is neutral on value questions, it doesn't say 'Tolerance is better than intolerance', any more than it says 'Intolerance is better than tolerance'. It leaves it to one's own point of view to decide. There is no more inconsistency in being an intolerant relativist than in being a tolerant one.

Bob: Frankly, I'm not sure what relativism *does* say. When I say witchcraft broke my leg, Zac doesn't openly agree or disagree, he just says 'That's your point of view'.

Zac: That *is* my point of view, Bob.

Bob: Be honest, Zac. Doesn't your point of view also say witchcraft *didn't* break my leg?

Zac: From my point of view, Bob, it didn't. But that's just my point of view.

Bob: Will you speak out like a man, and say witchcraft didn't break my leg?

Zac: I've already said, Bob: from my point of view, it didn't. Don't expect me to act all Clint Eastwood about it.

Bob: I'm not asking you to shoot me. I'm just asking whether you have the courage to say 'Witchcraft didn't break Bob's leg' without undermining your own words by adding that it's just your point of view?

Zac: Whenever I say anything, Bob, I am speaking from my own point of view.

Bob: But you agree, from my point of view, witchcraft did break my leg?

Zac: Yes, that's your point of view, Bob.

Bob: How do you know it's my point of view?

Zac: You just told me so, Bob.

Bob: I might have been lying. For all *you* know, I was just pretending to believe in witches.

Sarah: *Were* you just pretending?

Bob: No, of course not. I'm not that kind of person. But you and Zac have only my word to go on. You can't really know what's going on in my head.

Zac: OK, Bob. From my point of view: from your point of view, witchcraft broke your leg.

Bob: Are you sure you know what your own point of view is?

Zac: What's your problem, Bob?

Sarah: Actually, I think Bob may be on to something. It's not just knowing what's going on in someone *else's* head that's hard. Sometimes it's difficult to know what's going on in one's *own* head. Self-knowledge isn't always easy. For instance, people often make mistakes about whether they're in love. And I'm not clear what my point of view is on some of the things you've been saying, Zac.

Bob: Do you always know your own mind, Zac?

Zac: Bob, I don't claim to be better at that than anyone else.

Sarah: Sometimes I tell people I believe something, meaning to be honest, but afterwards I realize I didn't really believe that thing, even at the time. For example, when I was a little girl, I used to discuss with my friends whether the tooth fairy really existed. I remember announcing firmly to them that *I* believed in its existence. A couple of seconds later it dawned on me: for months, I hadn't really believed the tooth fairy existed. I knew perfectly well, it was my mum or dad who put the money under my pillow. Does that kind of thing happen to you too, Zac?

Zac: I'm just a human being, Sarah.

Sarah: That's what we suspected. So your opinions about your own opinions are fallible, like the rest of your opinions. Here's what's puzzling me. In an unguarded moment, you say witchcraft didn't break Bob's leg. When Bob challenges you on that, you retreat to saying *it is your point of view* that witchcraft didn't break Bob's leg. Bob may well agree that indeed that is your point of view. But suppose I start suspecting that you, Zac, don't really know your own mind and, deep down, you really believe in witches. So I challenge you on your claim that it is your point of view that witchcraft didn't break Bob's leg. I'm doubting that it is your real point of view. What would you say then?

Zac: That it is *my* point of view that it is my point of view that witchcraft didn't break Bob's leg, Sarah.

Sarah: Maybe you're not even as much of a relativist as you think you are. How do you know that relativism really *is* your point of view?

Zac: OK, Sarah, it is my point of view that relativism is my point of view.

Bob: I'm lost.

Sarah: What's going on, Bob, is that Zac has a standard tactic when he's faced with the threat of disagreement. He puts 'it's my point of view that...' in front of whatever he said before. Whenever you challenge one of his claims, he shifts to the different claim that his previous claim *is his point of view*.

Bob: I noticed that.

Sarah: He even does it with his claims about what his point of view is, when someone queries them. He retreats to saying it's his point of view on his own point of view.

Zac: I don't accept the word 'retreat', Sarah. I'd rather say 'advance', because I'm putting it on the table that it is just my own point of view.

Sarah: It's a retreat in the sense that you are backing off from what you first said and saying something about your own point of view instead. For instance, we were talking about what broke Bob's leg. It wasn't about you, Zac. We weren't talking about your point of view.

Zac: Each of us is just talking from his or her own point of view, Sarah. Do you want me to talk from someone *else*'s point of view instead?

Sarah: Talking *from* a point of view isn't the same as talking *about* it.

Zac: We should all be open and upfront about where we're coming from, Sarah.

Sarah: Yes, indeed, but one shouldn't use that as an excuse for changing the subject whenever it suits one and just talking about oneself. You have embarked on an endless, potentially infinite retreat. Every time you are challenged on one of your claims, you take another step backwards by putting another 'it is my point of view…' in front of what you last said, instead of standing by it. You don't have a stable position.

Zac: What's so good about stability, Sarah? We're all glad this train is moving nicely along, not standing stationary.

Sarah: That's different. This journey won't go on for ever. With a bit of luck, the train will take us to our destination. Your retreat has no destination, because you always take a further step back from any supposed destination when you come under pressure. To change the metaphor, you are trying to sell us this shiny new product, relativism.

Zac: That's not quite fair, Sarah. It's an ancient insight. There were relativists even in classical Greece, such as Protagoras.

Sarah: Well, if you prefer, you are trying to sell us this battered old product, relativism. We ask you what exactly we'd be buying. You tell us it is a point of view about points of view, that no point of view is absolutely right or absolutely wrong.

Zac: Yes, but hey, I'm not trying to *sell* it to you. I'm giving it to you free. There's no price to pay. If you find it useful, great. If you prefer not to use it, that's your decision.

Bob: If a garage made me a free offer of a car, I'd be scared to drive it. Who knows what might be wrong with the car?

Sarah: Anyway, there is a price to pay. We have to trade in our present car, absolutism, to get the other one.

Zac: It's your present one that kills, Sarah.

Sarah: I want to get back to my point. Someone suggests that the used car Zac is selling isn't as wonderful as he claims. Remember the criticism we talked about earlier. One should be able to apply relativism to itself, because it is a point of view about all points of view. Right, Zac?

Zac: Yes, Sarah, sure.

Sarah: Therefore relativism implies that relativism isn't absolutely right.

Zac: What's wrong with that, Sarah? It's still my point of view that no point of view, including relativism, is absolutely right or absolutely wrong.

Sarah: That's exactly what I'm complaining about. The car you are selling has a label on it: 'This car is no better than any other car'.

Bob: At least the salesman shows a sense of humour.

Zac: And modesty in his claims.

Sarah: A salesman who jokes that the used car he wants to sell you is nothing special may still be trying to cheat you. You ask whether the car actually starts and he changes the subject, starts talking about himself instead, how much *he* likes it. Do you buy the car?

Zac: You are welcome to a test drive.

Sarah: Even that could be dangerous.

Bob: I'm not sure I can even *see* the car. Zac shifts about so much, I don't know *what* he's trying to sell.

Sarah: Yes, whenever you try to get into a car to take it for a test drive, he says the one for sale is some-where else. If we buy relativism, we may be paying for nothing.

Zac: Cool it, guys. Let's all take a deep breath. One, two, three, four, five, aaaaaahhh. When I say something, and one of you responds by putting forward your own, different point of view—which is great—and then I say about what I first said 'It's my point of view', I'm not *withdrawing* what I first said. It's still there on the table. I'm just emphasizing that I'm not trying to impose my point of view on anyone. I'm not claiming what I said is absolutely right and whatever you guys said different is absolutely wrong. I'm saying I'm not trying to play God.

Bob: Why are you so scared we'll think you're trying to play God? When Sarah says something I disagree with, I know she's not trying to play God. She's just saying what she thinks. I'd never have thought you might be trying to set yourself up as God, Zac, if you didn't keep denying that you are.

Zac: I just don't want you to get the wrong impression, Bob. Plenty of sterile and hurtful disputes arise when not everyone accepts that different people have different points of view, and that it's fine for there to be such diversity.

Sarah: Indeed, but if so much of what you have been saying is just meant to remind Bob and me that we are all fallible human beings, which both of us knew very well already, then we are left still wondering what your relativism means. What can it be saying, if what it says doesn't exclude what anyone else might say? It's like saying 'The car is red, but you can equally well describe it as green, or blue, or yellow'.

Bob: An old hippy in my street drives a spray-painted car like that.

Sarah: It's not red all over *and* green all over. I need a less distracting way to make my point.

Zac: A colourless point.

Sarah: Let me try again. Can we express your relativism as 'Every point of view is just a point of view'?

Zac: In a sense, Sarah. We can talk that way if you like.

Sarah: If Bob says 'Witchcraft works' and I reply 'That's just your point of view', I'm refusing to endorse his statement. I'm accepting that it's his belief but by putting in the word 'just' I'm rejecting the idea that it's *more* than his belief, that witchcraft actually does work. In the same way, when Zac says something and then later says 'That's just my point of view', he sounds as if he's refusing to endorse his own earlier statement, disowning it. That's the retreat Bob and I complained about. But now Zac tells us he *isn't* disowning his earlier statements.

Zac: Exactly, Sarah.

Sarah: You're accepting that it's what you believe but you're *not* rejecting the idea that it's more than that. You are *adding* to what you previously put on the table, not *replacing* it. So we should delete the word 'just', because you don't really mean that it's *just* your point of view.

Zac: Delete it if you like, Sarah. The wording was yours, not mine.

Sarah: I will. So instead of saying 'Every point of view is *just* a point of view', relativism says 'Every point of view is a point of view'.

Zac: So it is.

Sarah: Yes, but that makes relativism utterly trivial! Everyone, even the most hard-line absolutist, will agree that every point of view is a point of view.

Zac: Sarah, you're trying to reduce relativism to a formula. It's not just one more theory, in competition with all the others. It's more like an attitude to life.

Bob: What attitude?

Sarah: Zac, you don't seem to behave very differently from many people in our society who wouldn't regard themselves as relativists. You're a fallible human being, like the rest of us, and you haven't massacred anyone, as far as we know, but even refraining from massacre is not such an unusual accomplishment. So what makes you a relativist, apart from your overuse of the phrase 'point of view'?

Zac: You know, Sarah, the difference is less in what relativists say but absolutists don't than in what relativists *don't* say but absolutists *do*.

Sarah: Such as?

Zac: I mean things involving dogmatic words like 'right' and 'wrong' or 'true' and 'false', Sarah. It's when people start throwing around those threatening words, and acting on them, that stuff happens, bad stuff: bombings, invasions, forcible conversions, massacres in the name of God or progress, like I was mentioning before. Relativism offers you the chance to avoid all that.

Sarah: So really we should start by trying to understand what *absolutism* says, not what relativism says, then we'll see what relativists want to avoid?

Zac: Now you're getting it, Sarah.

Sarah: Since the train is drawing into a station, Zac, may I non-forcibly convert you to the point of view that we should pause this conversation until the bustle of people getting off and on has subsided?

Zac: I share that point of view, Sarah.

Bob: Modern science and relativism agree on something.

{ PART II }

The Terrors of Truth

Zac: Ah, we are moving again at last.

Roxana: That is my seat you are sitting in.

Zac: Are you sure?

Roxana: I am. The number is written here on my reservation.

Zac: Sorry, let me remove my clutter.

Sarah: The seat next to me isn't reserved.

Zac: Thanks, Sarah, it suits me just as nicely.

Sarah: You were going to tell us, Zac, what you think is so bad about using absolutist words (as you put it) like 'true' and 'false'. Haven't I the right, even the duty, to speak out for the truth on the evidence, and say that it's *true* that witchcraft doesn't work, and *false* that it does?

Bob: Can't I say it's *true* that witchcraft works, and *false* that it doesn't?

Zac: I can't stop either of you saying those things. But here's why you might have second thoughts. Truth is supposed to be better than falsity, right, Sarah?

Sarah: Naturally.

Bob: Only fools prefer being wrong to being right.

Zac: So if you, Sarah, say your belief is true and Bob's is false, you imply that your belief is *better* than Bob's, and so, at least on this, *you* are better than Bob. And if you, Bob, say *your* belief is true and *Sarah's* is false, you imply that your belief is better than Sarah's, and so on this *you* are better than Sarah. Does either of you really want to claim superiority over the other?

Sarah: You make it sound so *personal*. The belief that witchcraft doesn't work is not my private possession. It's not just *my* belief. It's one I share with any scientifically educated person. And Bob's belief that witchcraft does work isn't just *his* belief. It's one he shares with other superstitious people, past and present. Questions of fact should be discussed in a more impersonal, objective way. Whether it's true or false that witchcraft works doesn't depend on what anyone believes.

Bob: You can't keep the personal side out of it entirely. When you say it's false that witchcraft works, you imply *you* believe it doesn't work. Otherwise you weren't being sincere.

Sarah: All right, but there's no need to make a fuss about it. The question is about witchcraft, not about you or me or Zac.

Bob: It's about me if I'm the victim of witchcraft.

Sarah: That concerns you as an item of evidence, a specimen case, not you as a party to the discussion.

Bob: Don't cut me in half. My personal experience of witchcraft is what gives me something to add to the discussion, something you others lack. We can't discuss witchcraft like it had nothing to do with us.

Zac: Debates have a personal edge in science too. Scientific reputations and ambitions are at stake.

If a scientist is judged to have designed an experiment well, his or her reputation goes up.

Bob: Glory.

Zac: Your word, Bob. And if he or she is judged to have designed it badly, his or her reputation goes down.

Bob: Humiliation.

Zac: Your word again. At any rate, funding and promotion depend on such things.

Sarah: Of course, and so they should, but to determine whether the experiment was designed well or badly one must examine its design impersonally and objectively. Judging the people involved comes afterwards, and should be equally objective.

Zac: But you agree, Sarah, if you say Bob's beliefs about witchcraft are false, and other people accept your judgement, that isn't good for Bob's reputation as someone who knows what he's talking about? He loses credibility.

Sarah: That isn't the issue.

Bob: It's an issue for me.

Zac: Sarah, when you think and say your belief is true and Bob's is false, there are consequences, for both you and Bob. You have to be careful.

Sarah: I *am* careful. I'm not saying that *whenever* Bob and I disagree, I'm right and he's wrong. I don't think for a moment I'm infallible. Bob knows more about gardening than I do. But I am right about witchcraft, and he is wrong.

Zac: You say so, Sarah, while admitting you're fallible?

Sarah: Yes. Science is all about learning from one's mistakes. Belief in witchcraft was one of many mistakes in the progress of humanity.

Zac: I'm curious, Sarah, to understand how you feel in a position to assert that you are right about something, and anyone who disagrees with you is wrong. Let's discuss that for a while. Do you think *all* your beliefs are true?

Sarah: No, I said, humans are fallible animals. It's normal to have many false beliefs. Why should I be an exception? I'm sure many of my beliefs are false.

Zac: Can you give an example, Sarah?

Sarah: I used to believe that Bob had a very conventional outlook on life. Now I find I was mistaken about that.

Zac: But what about your *present* beliefs? Are all of *them* true?

Sarah: No. Going on past experience, I'm sure many even of my present beliefs are false. The history of science is compelling evidence that many current scientific theories will have to be revised in the future, because so many scientific theories had to be revised in the past. Lots of our scientific theories must be false, although they may be good *approximations* to the truth. *I* can't credibly pretend to do better than *science*.

Zac: Go on, give us an example of one of your present false beliefs, Sarah.

Sarah: That's an unreasonable demand! If I knew *which* of my present beliefs were false, I'd abandon them, and they wouldn't be my present beliefs any more. 'Here's one of the falsehoods I believe: blah-blah-blah.' I'd look pretty silly saying that, wouldn't I? Some of my present beliefs must be false, but I don't yet know which.

Zac: So whenever I ask you about one of your present beliefs, Sarah, you'll say it's true, even though you admit that some of them are false. How consistent is *that*?

Sarah: Well, if we are going to be really accurate, it's like this. If you ask me about one of my present beliefs, I'll say it is *probably* true, on my evidence. Science works with probabilities, not with definitive proofs. Each of my beliefs is probable, I hope, even though it's not probable that *all* my beliefs together are true. That's perfectly consistent. It's like a lottery: before the draw is made, any given ticket will probably lose, even though of course it's not probable that the tickets will *all* lose. There has to be a winner.

Bob: So it's *not* certain witchcraft doesn't work. Admit it.

Sarah: Yes, it's not strictly certain, although it is *very* probable indeed that witchcraft doesn't work.

Bob: But less probable than that the three of us are sitting on a train, which we can see with our own eyes?

Sarah: On our evidence, it is even more highly probable that we are sitting on a train than that witchcraft doesn't work. Neither is *absolutely* certain.

Bob: At least you grant it's not *certain* I'm wrong.

Zac: Sarah, do you mean that modern science has substituted a scale of probabilities for the outdated dichotomy of truth and falsity?

Sarah: One could put it that way, I suppose.

Zac: I'm seeing more to like in your point of view, Sarah.

Sarah: I'm not saying that all theories are *equally* probable on the evidence. I'm saying that many have *non-zero* probability, but some are more probable than others. One can be less personal about disagreements once one realizes that one is only saying that one's point of view is more probable than one's opponent's, not that one is certainly right and he or she certainly wrong.

Bob: Are you still saying flat-out, witchcraft doesn't work, Sarah, or are you just saying it probably doesn't work?

Sarah: I'm saying that, on our evidence, it is very improbable indeed that witchcraft works.

Bob: Well, we still disagree, because I say that, on our evidence, witchcraft probably *does* work. Are you sure you've got the probabilities right, Sarah?

Sarah: Yes, I'm quite confident.

Bob: Have you never underestimated or overestimated a probability?

Sarah: Well, I'm not *infallible* about probabilities. When I lose at cards, I try to work out afterwards why. Sometimes I realize I estimated the probabilities incorrectly. Like Zac and you, I'm a human being. I'm fallible about everything.

Bob: You might be wrong about the probability that witchcraft works?

Sarah: In principle, yes, but in this case the improbability is very clear.

Bob: But when you say it's very improbable that witchcraft works, you agree it isn't *absolutely certain* that it's very improbable?

Sarah: Of course I agree: my judgements about the improbability, on our evidence, of witchcraft working are not absolutely certain. Nothing is. But it is *very* probable that it is very probable that witchcraft doesn't work.

Zac: Probabilities of probabilities, Sarah! You take this thing seriously, don't you? Next you'll be telling us about probabilities of probabilities of probabilities.

Sarah: In principle, yes.

Bob: This is starting to remind me of something. If I understood what you said to Zac, you want to think in terms of big and small probabilities, not truth and falsity.

Sarah: Yes, that's the general idea.

Zac: Welcome to the relativist club, Sarah! You are ditching the dogmatic words 'true' and 'false', just as I recommended.

Sarah: Don't be cheeky, Zac. I'm no relativist. Some estimates of probability are better than others.

Zac: Are you certain, Sarah?

Sarah: I have enough confidence to be getting on with, thank you.

Bob: You said before: since you can be wrong about things like witchcraft, you're not saying outright it doesn't work; you're just saying it's probable that it doesn't work. Since you can also be wrong about probabilities, as you just admitted, are you really saying outright that it's probable that witchcraft doesn't work, or are you just saying it's probable that it's probable that it doesn't work?

Sarah: I'm surprised that you of all people, Bob, should be so pedantic.

Bob: Don't blame me if I'm starting to get the hang of this game. Like you said before, we should stick to the issues, not personalities. How about answering my question?

Sarah: Since you insist on an answer, don't blame me if it's a complicated one. What I am asserting is that it is *very* probable that it is *very* probable that witchcraft doesn't work. I'm talking about probabilities on present evidence, of course. They were different on past evidence, when science was less developed, and they may be different on future evidence, once science has developed still further.

Bob: Now you remind me of Zac, the way he got into trouble before the last stop.

Zac: It was no trouble, Bob.

Bob: That's just your point of view, Zac. Whenever you said something, and Sarah or I pressed you on it, you backed off, and retreated to saying instead that what you first said was your point of view.

Zac: It was a clarification, Bob, not a retreat.

Bob: Call it a clarification if you want. From my point of view, Zac, you never stood your ground. Now, whenever Sarah says something, and you or I press her on it, she's started backing off, and saying instead that what she first said is very probable. 'It's very probable on present evidence' sounds scientific, while 'It's my point of view' sounds New Age, but they're both ways of shifting your ground. Sarah, have you really stopped sticking by what you say?

Sarah: I see what you mean, Bob. No offence, Zac, but I don't want to sound like you.

Zac: None taken, Sarah. I respect your different point of view. The more points of view, the better.

Sarah: Bringing in lots of *silly* points of view only causes confusion. Anyway, an infinite regress of probabilities of probabilities isn't much better than an infinite regress of points of view on points of view. I have to take a stand somewhere. I *will* say it outright. Witchcraft doesn't work.

Bob: That's what you thought all along.

Sarah: But I will *also* say outright: it is very probable that witchcraft doesn't work. No more retreating for me.

Zac: But you *do* sound like me, Sarah. First I put my point of view on the table. Then, while keeping it on the table (which is why it's not a retreat, Bob), I *also* put on the table that it is my point of view.

Sarah: The difference between us is that when you put on the table that what you first put on the table is your point of view, that's a redundant move, because we were all taking for granted anyway that it was your point of view. (It's not redundant if you say it's *just* your point of view, since that *withdraws* your endorsement from what you first said, but that's the retreat you say you're not making.) Now when I say something, and add that it's very probable, still standing by the original claim instead of backing off to talking *just* about probability, it's not redundant, because I'm actually *supporting* what I first said by appeal to probabilities on the evidence.

Bob: You're not giving up probabilities, are you?

Sarah: No, we still need them. Sometimes we can only make a statement about probabilities. Before I toss a fair coin, I can't say 'It will come up heads' and I can't say 'It will come up tails'. I can only say 'There's a 50% chance of heads and a 50% chance of tails'. But once I have tossed it and seen it come up heads, I have enough evidence to say 'It came up heads'. I don't need to confine myself to a statement about probabilities then. I'll take the same attitude to the statement 'Witchcraft doesn't work' too, because there's enough evidence.

Zac: So when you say 'Witchcraft doesn't work', Sarah, do you also say 'It's *true* that witchcraft doesn't work'?

Sarah: Saying that would sound rather dogmatic, I agree. I don't need to say 'true', I can just say 'very probable on the evidence' instead.

Roxana: You appear not to know much about logic.

Sarah: *What* did you say?

Roxana: I said that you appear not to know much about logic.

Sarah: And you appear not to know much about manners.

Roxana: If you want to understand truth and falsity, logic will be more useful than manners. Do any of you remember what Aristotle said about truth and falsity?

Bob: Sorry, I know nothing about Aristotle.

Zac: It's on the tip of my tongue.

Sarah: Aristotelian science is two thousand years out of date.

Roxana: None of you knows. Aristotle said 'To say of what is that it is not, or of what is not that it is, is false, while to say of what is that it is, or of what is not that it is not, is true'. Those elementary principles are fundamental to the logic of truth. They remain central in contemporary research. They were endorsed by the greatest contributor to the logic of truth, the modern Polish logician Alfred Tarski.

Bob: Never heard of him. I'm sure Aristotle's saying is very wise; I wish I knew what it meant.

Roxana: I see that I will have to begin right at the very beginning with these three.

Sarah: We can manage quite well without a lecture from you, thank you very much.

Roxana: It is quite obvious that you can't.

Zac: I'm afraid I didn't catch your name.

Roxana: Of course you didn't. I didn't say it.

Zac: May I ask what it is?

Roxana: You may, but it is irrelevant.

Bob: Well, don't keep us all in suspense. What is it?

Roxana: It is 'Roxana'.

Zac: Nice name, Roxana. Mine is 'Zac', by the way.

Bob: I hope our conversation wasn't annoying you.

Roxana: Its lack of intellectual discipline was only slightly irritating.

Bob: Sorry, we got carried away. Just to complete the introductions, I'm Bob, and this is Sarah.

Roxana: That is enough time on trivialities. I will explain the error in what the woman called 'Sarah' said.

Sarah: Call me 'Sarah', not 'the woman called "Sarah"', if you please.

Bob: 'Sarah' is shorter.

Sarah: Not only that. We've been introduced. It's rude to describe me at arm's length, as though we weren't acquainted.

Roxana: If we must be on first name terms, so be it. Do not expect them to stop me from explaining your error. First, I will illustrate Aristotle's observation about truth and falsity with an example so simple that even you should all be capable of understanding it. I will make an assertion.

Bob: Here goes.

Roxana: Do not interrupt.

Bob: I was always the one talking at the back of the class.

Zac: Don't worry about Bob, Roxana. We'd all love to hear your assertion. Silence, please, everyone.

Roxana: Samarkand is in Uzbekistan.

Sarah: Is that it?

Roxana: That was the assertion.

Bob: So that's where Samarkand is. I always wondered.

Roxana: Concentrate on the logic, not the geography. In making that assertion about Samarkand, I speak truly if, and only if, Samarkand *is* in Uzbekistan. I speak falsely if, and only if, Samarkand is *not* in Uzbekistan.

Zac: Is that all, Roxana?

Roxana: It is enough.

Bob: I think I see. Truth is telling it like it is. Falsity is telling it like it isn't. Is that what Aristotle meant?

Roxana: That paraphrase is acceptable for the present.

Sarah: In that case, isn't Aristotle's point utterly trivial?

Roxana: Once one has understood it, yes. Nevertheless, you violated it.

Sarah: Are you suggesting that I am mentally defective?

Roxana: No, I am not going that far. I simply point out that you violated an elementary principle of the logic of truth.

Bob: Sarah is a highly intelligent and very well-educated lady, Roxana. I don't think she'd do a thing like that.

Roxana: You do not think so, but she did.

Sarah: How?

Roxana: Pay attention, all three of you. First, Sarah said that witchcraft does not work. Then she denied that she had to conclude that it is true that witchcraft does not work. She was scared to use the word 'true'. But as Aristotle observes, to say of what is that it is, or of what is not that it is not, is true. So Sarah was wrong. Whoever says that witchcraft does not work *should* conclude that it is true that witchcraft does not work.

Zac: That's Sarah's problem, not mine, Roxana. She was the one who claimed to know best about witchcraft.

Roxana: Your confusion was more general. You advised abstinence from the words 'true' and 'false', because their use leads to controversial value judgements, that someone's beliefs are better than someone else's.

Zac: Rock on, Roxana. That's why we should stop using the T-word and the F-word.

Roxana: Such abstinence is futile. The source of the value judgements is the tacit assumption that it is better to tell it like it is than to tell it like it isn't (in Bob's colloquial terminology).

Bob: It's not everyone who knows how to use colloquial terminology.

Roxana: Be quiet. I will resume. On the tacit assumption that it is better to tell it like it is than to tell it like it isn't, your statement that witchcraft works entails that it is better to say that witchcraft works than to say that it does not work, for if witchcraft works then saying that witchcraft works is telling it like it is, and saying that witchcraft does not work is telling it like it isn't.

Sarah: But what about *my* statement that witchcraft does *not* work?

Roxana: By parallel reasoning, your statement entails that it is better to say that witchcraft does not work than to say that it works.

Sarah: Thank you.

Roxana: Therefore, given the tacit assumption, each statement entails that making it is better than denying it.

Sarah: What's your point?

Roxana: That such controversies about comparative value arise even without words like 'true' and 'false'. This one arose because Bob asserted that witchcraft works while Sarah denied that it does. Each of them was trying to tell it like it is about witchcraft. If telling it like it is beats telling it like it isn't, then truth beats falsity.

Zac: With a stick! The violence implicit in the language of truth and falsity!

Roxana: At my school, one was beaten for interrupting like that. I was saying, the words 'true' and 'false' merely enable the underlying preference for telling it like it is to be expressed in fewer words, as a preference for truth. They do not explain the preference. Sarah briefly neglected the logic of truth. Zac persistently flouted it in constructing his naïve, misconceived objection to the use of the words 'true' and 'false'.

Zac: You don't understand, Roxana. I refuse to play the conventional game with the words 'true' and 'false', so why should I be bound by its rules?

Roxana: The failure of understanding is yours. In criticizing absolutism, you were attempting to demonstrate the objectionable consequences of playing that game by its rules. Therefore you must follow those rules in order to draw out their consequences. Otherwise you are merely imposing your own capricious conclusions. Unless you learn how to play the game by its rules, you will never understand what is and what is not required in playing it.

Sarah: But what if someone—maybe Zac—rejects the assumption that telling it like it is beats telling it like it isn't?

Bob: There are white lies. It isn't always better to tell it like it is to a dying man.

Roxana: When you do not prefer telling it like it is over telling it like it isn't, you do not prefer truth over falsity, and your use of words like 'true' and 'false' need not lead you to the controversial value judgements.

Sarah: Roxana, although I find your manner repellent—you see, it is infectious—I suspect you have a point. As someone who approaches life in a scientific spirit, I do prefer truth, and I prefer it because I prefer telling it as it is.

Bob: So do I most of the time, and so do all decent folk, if I've understood what you and Roxana are on about. But something puzzles me. If being true to your husband means telling it to him like it is, then wouldn't a wife who kept sleeping with other men and telling her husband all about it in full, accurate detail count as being true to him?

Roxana: That is a different sense of 'true'. Being true to a man does not just mean telling him the truth. Do not confuse the issue.

Bob: Sorry.

Zac: But is your sense of 'true' the *true* sense of 'true', according to you, Roxana?

Roxana: No, both senses are legitimate, but only one is relevant to the conversation.

Zac: Who privileged one sense of 'true' above the other, or above all the others 'true' may have? Bob felt his sense was relevant, so it was relevant *to him*.

Roxana: He thought that it was relevant to the preceding discussion, but he was wrong. What is relevant is the sense of 'true' in contexts such as 'it is true that witchcraft does not work'. That sense does not concern the avoidance of promiscuity.

Bob: I wish I'd never brought up that example.

Sarah: Anyway, as I was starting to say, the preference for truth is the root of science. And Roxana's point applies to science. Zac was wrong. It's not *words* like 'true' and 'false' that matter. They are just conveniences.

Bob: Public ones?

Sarah: Shut up, Bob. What matters is telling things as they are. Where we use the word 'true' in science, we could do without it if we had to, without significant gain or loss. Instead of asking 'Is it true that some particles travel faster than the speed of light?', we could simply ask 'Do some particles travel faster than the speed of light?' The main issue is the same. The words 'true' and 'false' are not what do the work. 'It is false that some particles travel faster than the speed of light' amounts to 'No particles travel faster than the speed of light'. Instead of asking 'What are the fundamental truths about light?', we could just as well ask 'What are the fundamental properties of light?'

Roxana: Some signs of intelligence at last.

Sarah: You flatter me.

Bob: Maybe I see what Roxana and Sarah are getting at. Asking 'Is it true that there are witches?' is just like asking 'Are there witches?' If we're not allowed to ask whether it's true that there are witches, we're not allowed to ask whether there are witches.

Sarah: Exactly.

Zac: Whoa there, everyone, not so fast! Surely once you start using the word 'true' you imply *certainty*. You can't call something *true* unless it's certain, beyond doubt. If you don't want to imply certainty, don't say 'true'.

Roxana: The usual confusion.

Zac: It may be a confusion from your point of view, Roxana, but from my point of view it's an insight.

Roxana: My point of view is the correct one. To show that, I will present an example. Consider the total number of coins now on this train, in pockets and elsewhere. Nobody has counted them. Nobody knows whether the number is odd, or even. Nevertheless, the number *is* either odd or even, although we cannot say which.

Sarah: If it really mattered, we could find out which by an exhaustive search of the train.

Bob: At gunpoint.

Roxana: But in our current situation, when no search has been made, it is neither *certain* that the number is odd nor *certain* that the number is even.

Zac: So what, Roxana?

Roxana: Since the number *is* either odd or even, it is either *true* that the number is odd or *true* that it is even. Therefore something is true but not certain. Either 'The number of coins now on the train is odd' is an example of truth without certainty, or 'The number of coins now on the train is even' is. We know that one of those two sentences *is* an example, although we are not in a position to know which of them it is. Zac was incorrect in claiming that truth implies certainty.

Zac: I'm unhappy with your either-or logic, Roxana. Not everything is black or white. There are shades of grey in between.

Roxana: Logic does *not* entail that everything is black or white. It does entail that everything is black or not black, but shades of grey *are* black or not black, because they are not black. Logic also entails that everything is white or not white, but shades of grey *are* white or not white, because they are not white.

Zac: Why not let me liberate you from your cold world of black and white, and grey, Roxana? Why not join me in my warm multi-coloured world where all the points of view of the rainbow clash harmoniously?

Roxana: This one needs remedial lessons.

Sarah: Zac, don't mind her. I'll try to explain what I think she was getting at in a different way. Let me ask you a question. You'll see why in a minute. Is it true that there is life on other planets?

Zac: I've no idea, Sarah. Nobody knows—at least, not from my point of view.

Sarah: OK, but is it certain that there is life on other planets?

Zac: No, Sarah, it isn't. As I just said, nobody knows.

Sarah: There you are. Truth doesn't require certainty, even from your point of view.

Zac: Sarah, what are you talking about? *I* get to tell *you* what my point of view is. You can tell me what *your* point of view is. You don't get to tell me what *my* point of view is.

Roxana: Listen and learn. I will analyse the logic of Sarah's questions. If truth entails certainty, then *uncer*tainty entails *un*truth. Yes?

Zac: Yeah, OK, we can play those logic games if you insist, Roxana.

Roxana: I insist. Sarah's first question was 'Is it true that there is life on other planets?'; call that the *truth question*. Her second question was 'Is it certain that there is life on other planets?'; call that the *certainty question*. Your response to the truth question was 'I don't know'. Your response to the certainty question was 'No'. Do you accept that those were your responses?

Zac: Yeah, Roxana, they were, but where is all this heading?

Roxana: You do not treat truth and certainty as the same. Your responses to the truth question and the certainty question were not equivalent. 'I don't know' is quite different from 'No'.

Zac: They are both negative responses, Roxana. What's the big difference supposed to be?

Sarah: When you next have to apply for a visa, try responding to the question 'Have you ever been involved in smuggling drugs?' with 'I don't know' instead of 'No'. You will soon find out the difference.

Roxana: If you, Zac, inferred untruth from uncertainty, you would have answered 'No' to the truth question, since you answered 'No' to the certainty question. But you did not. Sarah's questions caught you out. They revealed that in practice even you do not take truth to require certainty.

Bob: Sarah one, Zac nil.

Zac: The referee must be blind. Sarah was way offside.

Roxana: No. The slow motion replay clearly showed that Sarah was onside. The goal was correctly given.

Zac: As I've been saying all along, Roxana, the words 'true' and 'false' make trouble.

Roxana: No, the trouble was your confusion of truth with certainty, not anything in the elementary logic of 'true' and 'false'. Sarah saw the point much faster than you did.

Sarah: Don't patronize me, Roxana.

Roxana: I merely stated a truth.

Bob: I've been wondering about something else. I don't just want to *speak* the truth out loud. I want to *think* the truth in my head too. Your Aristotle quote only mentioned truth and falsity in speaking. What about in thinking?

Roxana: The answer is obvious. Aristotle's principles generalize from speech to thought. Truth in speech is telling things as they are; truth in thought is thinking them as they are. Falsity in speech is telling things as they are not; falsity in thought is thinking them as they are not. In thinking that Samarkand is in Uzbekistan, I think truly if, and only if, Samarkand *is* in Uzbekistan; I think falsely if, and only if, Samarkand is *not* in Uzbekistan. Applying 'true' and 'false' to beliefs is as straightforward as applying them to statements.

Sarah: Yes, just as I try to tell the truth because I want to tell things as they are, I try to think the truth because I want to think things as they are. It's clear why people want to think truly in practical situations. Actions based on thinking things as they are have much more chance of achieving their goals than actions based on thinking things as they aren't.

Bob: That's too abstract for me.

Sarah: I'll give you an example. I was once walking in the mountains and got lost. It was all in cloud and I couldn't see a path amongst the rocks. There was supposed to be one safe way down. I thought it went along a narrow ridge. I followed that ridge but it just got steeper and steeper. I had to climb back up. It was hard. I slipped and almost fell a long way.

Bob: Would you have survived the fall?

Sarah: No.

Bob: You shouldn't go up mountains like that by yourself, Sarah. It's too dangerous.

Sarah: I enjoy it. I feel intensely alive when I'm by myself in the mountains. One has to be so alert. Anyway, that's not the point.

Bob: Which is?

Sarah: My false belief about the way down almost killed me. I wasn't thinking it like it was about the way down. Once I started thinking it like it was, I got down safely. My later true belief saved my life.

Bob: How did you find the way down?

Sarah: When I got back up to where I'd been before, I met another walker. She showed me the right way down. In situations like that, it's clear why we prefer people to tell it like it is rather than telling it like it isn't. I trusted her—I didn't have much alternative. I was tired, and it was starting to get dark. If she'd told me the wrong way, I'd have been in big trouble again. You see, successful actions are based on thinking things as they are.

Bob: Actions based on false assumptions don't always go badly. I met the love of my life when I mistook her for a shop assistant and asked her a question.

Sarah: You must tell me the story one day. Anyway, you are right: actions based on true beliefs aren't *guaranteed* to go better than actions based on false ones; but they're much more likely to. Actions based on false beliefs go well only by luck.

Zac: Perhaps Bob's so-called mistake was true in a deeper sense, Sarah.

Sarah: Are you saying that the love of Bob's life was a shop assistant in a deeper sense?

Bob: How dare you insult her, Zac! She was an artist, with an artist's soul.

Zac: I was talking at a deeper level, Bob. From my point of view, all this dry Aristotelian logic-chopping is sterile, trivial, and shallow. I find far more depth in Friedrich Nietzsche's insight that 'truths are illusions one has forgotten *are* illusions'.

Roxana: That is the sort of remark that passes for deep amongst those untrained in logic. But it may at least have the virtue of being true by its own standard: it is an illusion Zac has forgotten *is* an illusion—if he ever knew.

Bob: What did Nietzsche mean, Zac?

Zac: Bob, he was talking about the inability of language to express adequately how things are.

Bob: I can sympathize with that, I'm often lost for words.

Zac: Nietzsche wasn't. He was pointing to a deeper inadequacy, in language itself, Bob.

Bob: I'm confused. What did he mean by 'illusion'?

Zac: Bob, he meant something that appears to be so, but isn't so.

Roxana: That is precisely Aristotle's definition of falsity, applied to appearances.

Sarah: It sounds to me as though Nietzsche meant that the things we regard as true are not really true, because language is misleading.

Roxana: That is consistent with Aristotle's definition of truth.

Sarah: Anyway, if we don't expect too much from language, perhaps we can avoid being misled by it. When Bob says the love of his life was not a shop assistant, I don't treat that as a complete picture of her personality. What he said is true unless she *was* a shop assistant.

Bob: She was not.

Sarah: We know, Bob.

Zac: Sarah, why let Roxana pull you into old Aristotle's way of thinking? Roxana, why keep appealing to his authority? That guy defended slavery. He said some people, not including him, are fitted by nature to be slaves. We don't accept his authority in morals or politics or biology or physics. Why should we accept it in logic?—especially when he tries to enslave us all to truth.

Roxana: Modern logicians do not appeal to Aristotle's authority in logic. They accept some of his logical claims and reject others, on their own merits. They have found Aristotle's initial characterizations of truth and falsity an appropriate starting point for fruitful investigation. For logical purposes, there is no serious alternative to them.

Zac: In that case, logicians should lighten up and stop being serious. Look what happened to Aristotle. He was so serious about truth and falsity that he thought people like him can *own* others and exploit them as much as they want. People with 'true' beliefs get to be the slaveholders and people with 'false' beliefs get to be the slaves.

Roxana: Aristotle's views on slavery depended on his social circumstances, unlike his views on the logic of truth and falsity, with which they had no connection. His views on the logic of truth and falsity have withstood the test of time. His views on slavery have not.

Zac: Don't blame me if logicians haven't yet woken up to Nietzsche's challenge, Roxana. Anyway, why should students be forced to study Aristotle's philosophy? It could make those with slaves as ancestors feel uncomfortable. Shouldn't we be shunning his writings? Unless we shun them, to demonstrate publicly our abhorrence for his views on slavery and our solidarity with those students, aren't we condoning his attitude to slavery?

Bob: It was his point of view. The more points of view the better, you said.

Zac: I don't see the relevance of that here, Bob.

Bob: I don't see its irrelevance myself, but never mind.

Roxana: Logicians do not worship Aristotle. He was fallible like everyone else, as Sarah would say. They respect him as a great logician and philosopher, having evaluated his scientific achievements. Even though some of my ancestors were enslaved by invaders, I did not feel uncomfortable reading Aristotle. I knew that his views on slavery were typical of his time. How much scrutiny could Zac's adored Nietzsche withstand? He went mad. Does that mean that everything he wrote is mad?

Zac: Of course not, Roxana.

Roxana: Nietzsche described woman as 'weak, typically sick, changeable, inconstant'. Am *I* weak?

Zac: No, no.

Roxana: Knowing what Nietzsche wrote about them, some women students may feel uncomfortable having to read his books, although I do not. Should *his* work be shunned?

Zac: No, Roxana, of course I'm not suggesting that.

Roxana: Then keep your ill-considered proposals to yourself.

Sarah: I think we all accept that someone who acts or thinks very badly in some ways may still make great scientific discoveries or create great works of art. Human beings are complicated. Zac, if you keep trying to undermine logical principles by attacking other sides of people who proposed them, we'll suspect that you do so because you can't think of good objections to the logical principles themselves.

Zac: Well, Sarah, let's say for the sake of argument that after all it isn't words like 'true' and 'false' that do the damage, nor even the trivial Aristotelian logic that goes with them. Let's say that, by themselves, they are harmless. I'm still suspicious of the glib macho distinction between telling it like it is and telling it like it isn't.

Bob: When you ask the way, don't you want to be told it like it is, not like it isn't?

Zac: Bob, sometimes there are many ways to the same destination.

Bob: You still want to be told a way to *that* destination, not somewhere else.

Zac: Sometimes one finds a new destination. That happened to you in the shop, Bob.

Bob: I don't need reminding.

Roxana: As you pointed out, being told the truth is not always preferable in its effects to being told a falsehood, although it usually is. That does not undermine the *distinction* between being told things as they are and being told them as they are not.

Sarah: There is still a difference between arriving at your original destination and arriving somewhere else, even if you end up preferring the somewhere else.

Bob: I've sometimes been given such vague directions it was hard to say afterwards whether I'd been told it like it was or told it like it wasn't.

Zac: Who wants geometrically precise directions? The most useful directions are rough and ready ones. The most useful words are not mathematically precise. Since language is vague, and there are always borderline cases, what sense does it make to distinguish between telling it like it is and telling it like it isn't?

Roxana: Almost every distinction made in everyday language has borderline cases. They do not prevent distinctions from being of use, for instance that between bald and not bald. Some men are borderline cases, neither clearly bald nor clearly not bald. Nevertheless, since other men are clearly bald, and others clearly not bald, one can still use the word 'bald' in describing someone's appearance to those who have never met him.

Sarah: Bob is clearly not bald.

Bob: I'm relieved to hear you say that.

Sarah: That man at the other end of the carriage is clearly bald.

Zac: He will have gone bald gradually, Sarah. He didn't just wake up one morning and find all his hair had fallen out. He was borderline for years.

Bob: What about him down this end? He's doing his best with some long strands of hair, craftily wound over his scalp. Is he bald?

Sarah: Another borderline case.

Roxana: No, he is clearly bald.

Zac: It can be deeply hurtful to describe a man as bald, Roxana.

Sarah: We didn't mean *you*, Zac! You still have quite a bit of hair.

Zac: I didn't mean me, Sarah. I was talking generally. Distinctions are dangerous things. It's not nice to be always putting people in boxes. You talk about borderline cases. Making a distinction is dividing things into those on one side of the line and those on the other. You won't let them cross the line if they don't have a passport. It's the either-or logic that I've already objected to, the destructive craving for distinctions. We should spend less time dividing, and more time

Bob: Multiplying.

Zac: That too, Bob, but I was going to say joining.

Roxana: You relied on a distinction, in dividing dividing from joining.

Zac: Even when we have to make distinctions, Roxana, we shouldn't apply them with a judgemental attitude. Do you expect people to be grateful for being put into boxes? Those boxes may become coffins. *We* should thank *them* when they don't fit into our little boxes. They are reminding us that our distinctions are for us, not for them.

Bob: No idea what you're talking about.

Zac: Bob, we shouldn't regard our distinctions as *right*, and other people's as *wrong*. Different distinctions suit different purposes. Scientists classify materials by molecular structure, but an artist may classify them by colour.

Sarah: What about the Nazis' distinction between Aryans and non-Aryans, based on racial pseudo-science? It suited their purpose of creating scapegoats for persecution very well. Is it just as good as our distinction between humans and non-humans?

Zac: You know I'm not defending the Nazis, Sarah. Even so, they did have their own point of view. Historians have to understand it to make sense of their actions. Some people regard Nazis as sub-human, but that's a Nazi way of thinking. They were humans too.

Sarah: Is that an excuse, or part of the accusation? I see *you* classify them in the scientific way, by species, not the pseudo-scientific way, by race. It's science that finds the underlying fundamental distinctions.

Roxana: Sarah follows Plato. She hopes to cut nature at its joints.

Zac: You see, Sarah, distinguishing is butchery.

Bob: Butchers have a point of view too.

Sarah: If you prefer a more feminine metaphor, Zac, science needs the most *fruitful* distinctions. Biologists

try to find the most fruitful way to distinguish living beings into species.

Bob: You see, Zac, it is multiplication after all.

Sarah: And the mother of all distinctions is the distinction
between truth and falsity. When you draw a line,
you distinguish between the things of which it's
true that they are this side of the line and the things
of which it's false. Science needs distinctions, so it
needs the distinction between truth and falsity.

Bob: Witchcraft needs it too. It matters whether it's true
or false that someone is a witch.

Zac: Sarah, your argument went too fast for my eye
to follow. But even if a distinction between truth
and falsity is helpful in science, which I beg leave
to doubt, that doesn't make it needed, or helpful, or even meaningful, for the purposes of more
open-ended forms of human activity, outside
science.

Sarah: Achieving even non-scientific purposes usually
requires *action* of some kind. The action will probably fail if it's based on a false assumption. The
distinction between truth and falsity matters for
every purpose.

Zac: A confidently sweeping claim, Sarah. What does
the distinction between truth and falsity matter in
music?

Sarah: Composers and performers have purposes too. If
a composer wants to write a solemn, deeply moving piece, and thinks his score will sound that way,
but actually it just sounds irritatingly scratchy and
random, then he's failed in his purpose, because
he didn't think things as they were. If a performer

wants to play the notes in the score, but misreads it, he too has failed in his purpose, because he didn't think things as they were.

Zac: Sarah, some people may prefer the scratchy music, or the misread score.

Sarah: Even if they do, that's not the point. The composer and the performer still failed to achieve *their* purposes, because they worked on false assumptions.

Zac: What about truth in religion, Sarah? When someone says 'There is a God', they haven't made a statement that is true or false in a scientific sense.

Sarah: That's because the word 'God' has no scientific meaning.

Zac: It has meaning for the person who makes the statement.

Sarah: But can *we* understand it?

Zac: We can respectfully use *their* word 'God' to communicate with them.

Roxana: Then we can say: in stating that there is a God, they spoke truly if and only if there is a God, and falsely if and only if there is no God. Aristotle's principles apply just as well to religious statements as to scientific ones.

Zac: But the way religious people go about answering the question 'Is there a God?' is completely different from the way scientists go about answering their questions.

Sarah: So much the worse for religious people. They should take a scientific approach to answering their question, especially since it is such an important one.

Zac: If they tried to take a scientific approach, they wouldn't be playing the religious language-game, as old Ludwig would say.

Bob: Ludwig who?

Zac: Ludwig Wittgenstein, Bob. As he would say, the underlying grammar of the question 'Is there a God?' is quite different from that of the question 'Is there a boson?'

Roxana: According to linguists, 'Is there a God?' and 'Is there a boson?' have the same grammatical structure, in both syntax and semantics.

Bob: I don't know much about grammar, but I can't see what difference you're getting at, Zac. And I don't think my religious friends would like being told their religion is just a game.

Zac: I don't think you've understood how Wittgenstein was using the words 'game' and 'grammar', Bob.

Bob: Why couldn't he speak in ordinary language? From what you say, he used everyday words like 'grammar' as his own technical jargon.

Zac: Bob, he was talking about a deeper sort of grammar than linguists study.

Roxana: Zac is one of those who think a muddy river deeper than a clear one, because they cannot see the bottom.

Zac: I'd love to psychoanalyse your choice of metaphors, Roxana.

Roxana: Do not project your dirty thoughts onto me.

Sarah: Psychoanalysis was scientifically discredited decades ago.

Zac: It's not meant to be a science, Sarah. It's an open-ended method of interpretation.

Sarah: Or misinterpretation.

Roxana: Is Zac willing to listen to what I have to say without disrupting it with his irrelevant associations?

Zac: Is their irrelevance relevant, Roxana?

Roxana: No more delaying tactics. Zac appeared to assume that if people use different methods to answer a question, they mean different things by it. He denied that the words 'true' and 'false' mean in religion what they mean in science, because they are applied on the basis of different methods.

Zac: That's what a difference in meaning *is*, Roxana.

Roxana: No, you are confusing meaning with method of verification. Two people may use different methods to determine when to apply a word, yet still mean the same by it.

Bob: I'm lost again.

Roxana: When DNA tests were first used in murder trials, the meaning of the word 'murderer' did not change.

Zac: That's only a difference of degree. It's not like the radical difference in kind between religious and scientific ways of answering a question.

Sarah: Even they can answer the same question. A religious person and a scientist may agree on what sort of character and powers it takes to be a God, but then go about trying to find out whether there is one in radically different ways. One uses prayer, the other experiment.

Bob: Isn't prayer a sort of experiment—waiting to see whether it gets answered?

Sarah: Perhaps, but it's not a properly controlled experiment. No scientific journal would accept it for publication.

Zac: Even if we say the question 'Is there a God?' is the same, the answer depends on the point of view from which it is answered. It may be 'No' from the point of view of a scientist, 'Yes' from the point of view of a religiously inclined person.

Sarah: Your talk about points of view collapsed before the last station.

Bob: With much less collateral damage than my wall.

Sarah: Yes, Zac just means that the scientist *thinks* the answer is 'No' while the religious person *thinks* the answer is 'Yes'. The question is which answer is *true*, and which is *false*. That just depends on whether there *is* a God.

Zac: Don't you regard those who give the so-called right answer as somehow *better people* than those who give the so-called wrong answer?

Sarah: Not automatically. We can discuss who's right and who's wrong on a question without committing ourselves to who's righteous in general and who isn't. In practice, though, people who take a scientific approach have a much better chance than others of finding the true answers to questions, because they are intellectually honest, they look at all the evidence, and they don't indulge in wishful thinking. They don't believe in an afterlife just because they are scared of dying.

Zac: Is that a scientifically drawn self-portrait, Sarah?

Sarah: I don't pretend always to live up to my own ideals. Do as I say, not as I do. But by *aiming* at those ideals, scientifically minded people are likely to do better than those who don't even *try*.

Zac: Sarah, that sort of complacent faith in Western science is part of the reason why Western societies regard themselves as *systematically* right, and non-Western societies as *systematically* wrong, wherever their points of view diverge. That attitude makes Western societies assume they have the right to bomb and invade non-Western societies, to put them to rights—by Western standards.

Sarah: I regard myself as systematically right, and Bob as systematically wrong, over a wide range of scientific matters, but that doesn't make me think I have the right to invade his house in order to re-educate him.

Zac: Sarah, you might feel differently if you were much stronger than Bob, and the local police were as ineffective as the United Nations.

Sarah: That's unfair. Tolerance of other opinions, even utterly wrongheaded ones—

Bob: Thanks!

Sarah: (I didn't just mean you, Bob)—as I was saying, tolerance is central to my code of values. It is crucial for science, to allow revolutionary new theories to emerge.

Bob: Don't be too sure, Zac, that Roxana won't invade *your* house to re-educate you in logic.

Roxana: I doubt that Zac is re-educable in logic.

Zac: You are welcome to try, Roxana.

Roxana: Even if you are re-educable, which is highly unlikely, I have not the least desire to enter your house. You will have to find someone else to re-educate you there.

Sarah: To get back to the point, I completely reject Zac's idea that insisting on the difference between truth and falsity leads to dogmatism. Remember, truth isn't certainty. Science insists on the difference between truth and falsity, but the scientific spirit also makes us self-critical and tolerant of contrary opinions, because we are all fallible. Whenever one asserts something, one should be willing to add 'but I may be wrong'. The person one is disagreeing with may be right after all. In that sense I call myself a 'fallibilist'. It's the very importance of the distinction between truth and falsity that should make us humble, and tolerant of others. It is bigger than all of us.

Zac: In other words, Sarah, you say 'There are no witches, but since I may be wrong about that, I won't force Bob to agree with me'?

Sarah: Yes, science flourishes on diversity of opinions. Competing theories all have their own supporters, so each theory is tried out properly, to discover what it can explain, and what it can't. Through that process, we eventually find out which theory is best, of those we are comparing. Even when we accept the best of them, we still add 'but we may be wrong', because there may be a still better theory nobody has thought of yet. There is massive evidence in favour of theories that postulate electrons, but conceivably one day those theories will be replaced by theories that postulate something else instead.

Zac: Exactly, Sarah, in the middle ages, people knew the sun goes round the earth. Now we know differently from them. We know there are electrons, but in a thousand years people may know differently from us.

Roxana: Yet another standard elementary error. The medievals did *not* know that the sun goes round the earth. They only *thought* they knew. One knows that something is so only if it *is* so. The sun does not and never did go round the earth. The medievals *thought* that the sun goes round the earth, but they were wrong. They also thought that they knew that the sun goes round the earth, but they were wrong about that too.

Sarah: I agree with you there, Roxana. Religion gives belief but not knowledge. Science gives knowledge, because it is properly tested, even though it never achieves certainty.

Bob: I agree with Roxana too. Sarah *believes* witchcraft doesn't work, but she doesn't *know* it doesn't work.

Roxana: What matters is the logical point. Only truths are known. Both truths and falsehoods are believed.

Bob: That makes sense to me.

Zac: In tying the word 'knowledge' to the word 'truth', as you absolutists do, you infect 'knowledge' with all the sickness of 'truth'.

Bob: What sickness?

Zac: Bob, I'm talking about the problem of power, which uses violence to enforce what it calls the distinction between truth and falsity. By linking 'knowledge' and 'truth', power also uses violence to enforce what it calls the distinction between knowledge and ignorance.

Sarah: I don't use violence to enforce anything!

Zac: Your taxes help pay for an army to do it for you, Sarah.

Sarah: I didn't vote for any invasions.

Zac: This isn't just about you, Sarah. Knowledge is power. Truth is politics by other means.

Bob: If I have to choose either knowledge and power or ignorance and impotence, I know which *I'll* take.

Sarah: There are good and bad ways of using knowledge. We have a better chance of avoiding the worst ways if we are fallibilists, accepting that anyone can be mistaken about anything. Fallibilism makes us more tolerant of other people and other cultures.

Zac: Does it imply that all cultures are equal in truth and knowledge, Sarah?

Sarah: No, that would be ridiculous. Of course scientifically advanced cultures have more knowledge than primitive ones. You yourself assume that different cultures are unequal in power. If knowledge and power are the same thing, as you seem to think, doesn't it follow that different cultures are unequal in knowledge too?

Bob: If the President of the United States of America has the most power in the world, does he also have the most knowledge?

Zac: When I say 'Knowledge is power', Bob, I'm using a subtler concept of identity.

Roxana: No, just a more confused one.

Zac: Knowledge makes power and power makes knowledge. Hey guys, it's complicated.

Bob: Chickens make eggs and eggs make chickens.

Sarah: At first, Zac, you said that relativism implies tolerance. But that didn't work because, for you relativists, moral values like tolerance depend on one's point of view, like anything else. A relativist can invade other countries if that's a good idea from his point of view.

Zac: From my point of view, Sarah, it's a very bad idea.

Sarah: I know. I'm not accusing you personally of being a major threat to world peace. But it's fallibilism, not relativism, that gives us pause by reminding us we may be wrong. It emphasizes the risk that we are acting on false beliefs. Relativism dismisses that risk, because the beliefs are not false from the point of view of the believer.

Zac: Aren't the assumptions behind a plan *not* to invade just as fallible as the assumptions behind a plan *to* invade, Sarah?

Sarah: Yes, but awareness of our fallibility tends to make us cautious. Not invading is a more cautious option than invading.

Bob: Would a fallibilist Supreme Commander of Allied Forces in Europe in 1944 have ordered the Normandy landings not to go ahead?

Sarah: I suspect that a fallibilist Supreme Commander would have looked at all the available evidence, perhaps after having had more gathered, and then given the order for the landings to go ahead.

Bob: So how much difference does fallibilism actually make?

Sarah: Perhaps the actual Supreme Commander, Eisenhower, *was* a fallibilist, at least in practice, and acted just as a fallibilist should have.

Bob: Couldn't a relativist have taken Eisenhower's point of view, and acted the same way too?

Sarah: But it's fallibilism, not relativism, that encourages us to gather more evidence before taking our decisions. Fallibilism doesn't mean we should wallow in our mistakes, or not try to correct those we can. Better evidence makes for better decision-making.

Zac: If fallibilism looks so great, Sarah, then many relativists may adopt it, not as the absolute truth, but as their point of view. Then, when they make a decision, the best option from their point of view will be the best option from a fallibilist point of view. They will end up doing just what a fallibilist would do.

Roxana: That was the noise of Zac shooting himself in the foot. His argument for relativism was that accepting it has better practical consequences than accepting absolutism. Now he argues that accepting relativism can have the *same* practical consequences as accepting one form of absolutism, Sarah's fallibilism.

Zac: Roxana, why assume that fallibilism entails absolutism? Why not combine fallibilism with relativism, and have the best of both worlds?

Roxana: Fallibilism says that any of our beliefs may be false. Relativism rejects words like 'false'. How do you plan to combine them?

Zac: By taking the heart of fallibilism.

Roxana: And leaving the head.

Sarah: Thanks for the offer, Zac, but I'm afraid I don't trust you as a heart surgeon. It sounds as if my beloved fallibilism might not survive the operation. It's better off keeping head and heart together.

Zac: Sometimes only drastic surgery will save the patient, Sarah.

Sarah: Fallibilism doesn't need surgery. Just as it is, it fits nicely together with absolutism.

Roxana: Is fallibilism fallible?

Sarah: Of course it's fallible! That doesn't mean it's false.

{ PART III }

The Advantages of Arrogance

Bob: Watch out, that woman in black who walked past may be a witch! She looks like one to me. When she comes back, don't let her pick up one of your hairs as she passes. She could use it to put a spell on you.

Sarah: Oh, Bob, do stop all that nonsense! Of course she's not a witch. She was just going to use the lavatory.

Roxana: According to you, Sarah, she may be a witch.

Sarah: Don't be absurd. That's Bob's foolish idea, not mine.

Roxana: You call yourself a fallibilist. According to you, anyone may be wrong about anything.

Sarah: So?

Roxana: So according to you, you may be wrong that she is not a witch.

Sarah: In principle, yes, but it's *very* unlikely.

Roxana: But if you *are* wrong that she *is* not a witch, it follows that she is a witch.

Sarah: A big 'if'!

Roxana: So according to you, since *you* may be wrong that *she* is not a witch, she may be a witch.

Sarah: All right, she may be a witch, but that's *very* unlikely too.

Roxana: Therefore you were wrong to deny that, according to you, she may be a witch.

Sarah: You needn't rub it in.

Bob: Careful, she's coming back. Look at the sun shining on those hills.

Roxana: The sight is unremarkable.

Bob: She's gone. Did you notice how she put her hand on Zac's seat as she passed?

Zac: She was steadying herself as the train swayed, Bob.

Bob: She could have picked up a hair without your noticing.

Zac: Bob, I'll just have to take that risk.

Bob: Do you still deny she's a witch, Sarah?

Sarah: Yes. She's no witch. Period.

Bob: You risk saying it outright?

Sarah: Yes, I do. I said before, I have to take a stand somewhere. Life is a risky business. Risking being wrong is the price of being right.

Bob: But you admitted to Roxana, she may be a witch.

Sarah: Yes, what's the problem? That's my fallibilism.

Roxana: When Bob accuses that woman of witchcraft, you say 'She is innocent, but she may not be innocent'.

Zac: That won't sound very convincing, Sarah.

Sarah: But it's true!

Bob: Saying 'She's innocent, but she may not be', you give with one hand, then take back with the other.

Sarah: You have a point. It does sound odd, as if I'd lost my nerve half-way through the sentence. Perhaps I shouldn't have asserted outright 'She is innocent' in the first place.

Roxana: The problem is general because your fallibilism is general. It undermines any outright assertion you make about anything.

Sarah: Couldn't I assert outright 'It is very probable that she is innocent'?

Roxana: You have already admitted, you are fallible about probabilities.

Sarah: Yes, of course.

Roxana: Therefore you will have to say 'It is very probable that she is innocent, but it may not be very probable that she is innocent'.

Sarah: That sounds bad too, doesn't it?

Zac: I'm afraid I can't recommend you to her as a defence lawyer, Sarah.

Sarah: The problem is asserting something outright, then adding that it may not be so. It doesn't matter what it's about, even probabilities. Perhaps one simply shouldn't assert things outright.

Roxana: Do you assert that one should not assert?

Sarah: No, that would be condemning myself out of my own mouth, wouldn't it? I'd better just *conjecture* that one shouldn't assert.

Roxana: Sarah has a commitment problem.

Bob: Can you still think things straight out, Sarah?

Sarah: We're all just as fallible in thought as in speech. One should be willing to add 'but I may be mistaken' to whatever one thinks too. The problem is the same. Just as we shouldn't assert outright, we shouldn't think outright either.

Bob: You said you had to take a stand somewhere. Where are you taking a stand now?

Sarah: Nowhere, if taking a stand means being dogmatic about it. Whatever I think or speak, treat me as just conjecturing.

Bob: I'd never thought of you as indecisive. How will you ever make up your mind what to do, if all you have are conjectures? How will you decide when to get off the train?

Sarah: I'll just have to go on the probabilities.

Bob: You mean conjectures about probabilities?

Sarah: I'll have to rely on some of my conjectures. I'm more confident of some of them than of others. I'm pretty confident about which station to get off at.

Bob: You conjecture you're pretty confident.

Sarah: I'm pretty confident I'm pretty confident.

Roxana: Did you board this train unthinkingly, or had you reasoned what to do?

Sarah: Obviously I didn't just pick this train at random. I checked the platform. If you really analysed my thought processes, I suppose you'd find I reasoned from conjectures about the reliability of station announcements and so on to the conclusion that I should board this train.

Roxana: You relied on the conjecture that it was the right train.

Sarah: Or on the conjecture that it was very probable that it was the right train.

Roxana: In any case, you relied on conjectures.

Bob: Where's all this going?

Roxana: Without patience, you will never understand. What difference does Sarah suppose between thinking something outright and relying on it as a conjecture in deciding what to do?

Sarah: The difference is, I'm willing to add 'I may be mistaken'.

Roxana: You are just thinking things outright but adding the words 'I may be mistaken'.

Sarah: The addition is crucial. It keeps me humble.

Roxana: In practice your decision is the same, because it depends on the assumptions of your reasoning, not on your admission of fallibility. You still board the train, but in a humble manner.

Sarah: I often check my assumptions.

Roxana: Even if one thinks something outright, one can still check it, to be safe. It appears that your practice does not and could not comply with your new resolution never to think outright. Adding 'but I may be mistaken' is just a salve to your conscience for violating your impractical principles. Since you banned outright assertions, you have made many. You just asserted outright that you often check your assumptions. You made more assertions in boasting of your humility.

Sarah: I may be wrong about my humility!

Roxana: When a Roman emperor rode in triumph through the streets of the city, a slave stood behind him in the chariot to whisper in his ear reminders of his mortality, to keep him humble. It is doubtful how much effect those reminders had. The fallibilist is like that slave, whispering to us worthy but routine and largely futile reminders of our human fallibility.

Sarah: That's unfair. A fallibilist's reminders are quite specific. Every single thing we think, we are physically and psychologically capable of thinking when it is false. Although I think this is my train, I am physically and psychologically capable of thinking it's my train when in fact it isn't.

Roxana: A typically rash generalization. Are you physically and psychologically capable of thinking that you exist, when in fact you do not exist?

Sarah: That's a special case. Of course I'm not physically and psychologically capable of thinking without existing.

Roxana: Are you physically and psychologically capable of thinking that you think, when in fact you don't think?

Sarah: No. If I *think* I think, that *is* thinking.

Roxana: Are you physically and psychologically capable of thinking that you are fallible, when in fact you are infallible?

Sarah: No human is physically and psychologically capable of being infallible. Anyway, an infallible being couldn't be wrong about its own infallibility, I suppose.

Roxana: Are you physically and psychologically capable of thinking that 5 + 7 is 12 when in fact 5 + 7 is something else?

Sarah: No, 5 + 7 could not have been anything but 12.

Bob: People could use '+' to mean multiplication instead of addition.

Roxana: Obviously, but in those circumstances 5 + 7 would still be 12, not 35. The *signs* '5 + 7' would merely mean something other than 5 + 7. Do not confuse the issue again.

Bob: Sorry.

Sarah: I see. I was wrong that whatever we think, we are physically and psychologically capable of thinking it falsely. We're not always fallible in quite the way I thought. But I'm still a fallibilist, I admit my mistakes and learn from them. I withdraw my mistaken generalization. Fallibilism makes a more abstract point: humans are physically and psychologically capable of error in any area of thought. Even in mathematics, we can miscalculate.

Roxana: So fallibilism is just a general reminder of human fallibility, as I said.

Bob: Sometimes I think I've calculated correctly, but it turns out later I'd miscalculated. When I do calculate correctly, how do I know I'm not miscalculating?

Sarah: How bad a calculator are you? If you are really bad, maybe you don't know you are calculating correctly—even when you do get the right answer, you get it just by good luck.

Bob: I'm not that bad. I usually get it right.

Zac: Couldn't your memory be deceiving you about that, Bob?

Bob: I may be a worse calculator than I think.

Roxana: Even a perfect superhuman calculator with a perfect memory can say to itself 'I may be a bad calculator with a bad memory who just seems to itself to be a perfect calculator with a perfect memory'. Does that show that it does not know that 5 + 7 is 12?

Sarah: This is getting ridiculous. Unless knowledge is impossible, a good calculator must know that 5 + 7 is 12. The point of fallibilism is to set a standard for knowing that animals like us can actually reach. It's meant to make human knowledge possible. To set a standard that rules out all knowledge would defeat its purpose. If we calculate properly, we learn that 5 + 7 is 12, even though we can still torture ourselves with fanciful doubts.

Zac: Are you feeling sado-masochistic, Sarah? You get the pleasure of being tortured *and* the pleasure of torturing.

Sarah: Speak for yourself, Zac.

Roxana: Sarah reluctantly admits that she knows that 5 + 7 is 12.

Sarah: Yes. By normal human standards I can calculate correctly. I know that 5 + 7 is 12.

Roxana: Do you still add 'but I may be wrong that 5 + 7 = 12'?

Sarah: Perhaps I shouldn't. If I may be wrong that 5 + 7 is 12, I don't know 5 + 7 is 12. But I *do* know. We shouldn't cheapen 'I may be wrong' by saying it too easily. Making 'I know' too hard and 'I may be wrong' too easy are two sides of the same coin. It's pointless to set a standard for 'I know' we never meet, and equally pointless to set a standard for 'I may be wrong' we always meet. Why set a test it's impossible to pass, or one it's impossible to fail?

Zac: One of my most brilliant teachers gave an A to everyone who took his course, Sarah.

Sarah: He wanted to be popular.

Zac: He was, but for his inspirational, idiosyncratic, iconoclastic lectures.

Sarah: They sound irritating. How often did he say 'I may be wrong'?

Zac: He didn't use that vocabulary, Sarah, but I've never met anyone more open-minded.

Sarah: Well, I do use that vocabulary, but not indiscriminately. I won't say 'I may be wrong that $7 + 5 = 12$'.

Roxana: At last Sarah gives up her self-righteous display of intellectual humility.

Sarah: No one will ever accuse *you* of intellectual humility.

Roxana: I accused you of self-righteousness, not humility.

Bob: So what do you conclude, Sarah?

Sarah: We needn't be perfect to get knowledge. We can use our normal human powers of perception and reasoning properly, in normal circumstances. We shouldn't be ashamed to admit we have knowledge. But we also shouldn't forget we are only human.

Zac: Human, all too human.

Sarah: Judge human knowledge by human standards. Science has given us plenty of it. It's built on knowledge we gain by using our human senses to observe the world.

Zac: So what do you know by observing the world right now, Sarah?

Sarah: All four of us know that the sun is shining. We can see it.

Zac: Can you prove to me that we aren't hallucinating, Sarah?

Bob: Sarah doesn't have to prove anything to you, Zac.

Zac: It's not just to me, Bob. If speakers don't hold themselves accountable to others in making knowledge claims, they are being authoritarian. You can't tell others to accept your knowledge claim without giving them the chance to challenge you. *Anyone* is allowed to say 'Prove it to me, if you want me to accept your claim'. If Sarah isn't willing to play that game, she shouldn't go round making knowledge claims.

Sarah: I *am* willing to play that game. As a scientist, this time I agree with Zac.

Zac: Crack open the champagne!

Sarah: Let's stay sober, Zac. We still have many disagreements. But accepting statements on authority is anti-scientific. Science compensates for human fallibility by keeping all statements open to challenge.

Roxana: Shall I challenge that statement?

Sarah: What do you know about science, Roxana?

Zac: That sounds suspiciously like an appeal to authority, Sarah.

Sarah: I only asked Roxana a question.

Bob: Did you see, Sarah, that woman in black went past again?

Sarah: She's just gone to the lavatory.

Bob: So soon after the last time. What's she doing in there? She's up to no good.

Sarah: A girl's got to do what a girl's got to do.

Roxana: She's no girl.

Bob: What was she carrying in her handbag? Ingredients? My instinct says she's a witch.

Sarah: We all know she's no witch. Well, maybe you don't, Bob, but that's just your perversity.

Bob: Did you call me a pervert?

Sarah: I only meant, but for your eccentric views, you too would know she's no witch.

Zac: Sarah, can you *prove* to Bob she's no witch?

Sarah: Can anyone change Bob's mind on witchcraft? Bob, is there anything we can do when she comes back to test whether she's a witch?

Bob: That could be very dangerous. Never cross a witch.

Sarah: I'm willing to take the risk. If she *were* a witch, and I asked to look into her handbag, what would she do?

Bob: She'd not let you look into it. Later, she'd put a curse on you.

Roxana: I too would not let Sarah look into my handbag, but I am not a witch.

Bob: We've only your word for that.

Sarah: Here she comes.

Zac: She may have very intimate items in her handbag, Sarah.

Bob: Sarah, don't do anything! It's too risky.

Sarah: Excuse me, this will sound absurdly intrusive, but would you mind letting me look into your handbag? It's for a bet....Thank you, that's very kind....I win.

Zac: What was in it?

Sarah: A magnificent collection of cosmetics.

Bob: She didn't say a word. That's suspicious. Did you see the way she looked at you, Sarah? Who knows what she's done to you? Do you feel OK?

Sarah: I feel great, thanks. You must admit now, Bob, she's no witch. You said, if she were a witch and I asked to look into her bag, she'd refuse to let me. I did ask, and she let me look. So, by your own test, she's not a witch.

Bob: I may have been wrong about what a witch would do when asked.

Sarah: Oh, Bob, how can you? Anyway, what she had in the bag was totally innocent.

Bob: It *looked* innocent, I'm sure. A skilful witch could make her materials look just like ordinary cosmetics. Sarah, you may be in much deeper trouble than I thought. Speaking selfishly, I'm glad I'm not in your shoes.

Sarah: You see what I mean, Zac, about changing Bob's mind?

Zac: You are certainly determined to stick to your point of view, Bob. And *you* can't prove to Bob he's wrong, Sarah.

Sarah: By reasonable standards, I still *know* he's wrong and she's no witch. I even proved it by Bob's own standards, until he moved the goalposts. My inability to persuade *him* doesn't mean *I* don't know. It just means *he's* obstinate.

Bob: By reasonable standards *I* know she's a witch. I could really feel it as she stood there.

Sarah: Bob, knowing isn't just about your personal feelings. It's about what you can prove by standards other people can check. That's the scientific method.

Bob: Don't I count as other people? When I told you your proof didn't work, because it relied on my mistake about what a witch would do, you wouldn't accept my correction. What's so scientific about that?

Sarah: The checks have to be carried out by competent judges, not just by any old person who walks in off the street.

Bob: So now I'm just any old person?

Sarah: Nothing personal, Bob, but if scientific results had to be unanimously certified by everyone, one crank could hold up progress for ever.

Bob: 'Crank'!

Zac: Who gets to decide who's a competent judge and who's a crank, Sarah?

Sarah: The scientific community itself.

Zac: You mean, the people already certified as competent judges, Sarah?

Sarah: Yes, in effect. It takes one to know one.

Zac: Sarah, what you're saying is this. The scientific community is a self-perpetuating elite. The rest of us must simply accept their authority. They have to justify their scientific statements to each other, but not to us. Isn't that a pretty authoritarian set-up?

Sarah: The scientific community isn't closed. Anyone can join, if they prove themselves competent by getting a scientific education and passing the exams.

Zac: Prove themselves competent *to those already in that community*, Sarah. You're telling Bob that your knowledge claim counts and his doesn't because you belong to the scientific club and he doesn't. Isn't your knowledge claim just a fig leaf for naked power?

Bob: Look at that dog down the carriage. He's wagging his tail because he knows he's about to be fed.

Roxana: As usual, Bob's attention wanders.

Sarah: Is Bob's claim of knowledge for the dog a fig leaf for naked power too, Zac?

Zac: You've got it, Sarah.

Bob: Whose naked power? The dog's?

Zac: No, *yours*, Bob. Humans decide what dogs know. Dogs have no say in the matter.

Bob: You don't have to like my clothes, but don't call me naked.

Zac: I love your clothes, Bob. But it's the clothed who get to decide what the unclothed know, just like scientists get to decide what non-scientists know.

Roxana: Now 'naked power' has put on proper clothes.

Bob: I have a fig tree. One of *its* leaves wouldn't keep you warm. It wouldn't even keep you decent.

Sarah: Anyway, we humans may judge what animals know, but our judgements can be wrong. Look, that dog didn't know he was about to be *fed*. He's *drinking* from the bowl. What he knew was that he was about to be given water.

Zac: That's a human correction of a human judgement, Sarah.

Bob: Now he knows there is water in his bowl. He can see it and taste it.

Roxana: Can the dog prove to competent judges that there is water in his bowl?

Sarah: Dogs can't justify their beliefs to anyone. It would be silly to expect them to. But they still know things, using their senses.

Bob: If dogs know without proof, why can't humans?

Zac: We can talk and they can't, Bob.

Sarah: If a human claims to know something, I can demand proof. If they can't produce one, I reject the knowledge claim. Humans can be expected to meet the demand for proof, since they understand the challenge. Dogs don't, so they can't be expected to meet it.

Bob: Are you saying, since we can talk and dogs can't, it's harder for us to know than for them? We have to be able to answer questions; they don't. You'd expect language to make knowing easier, not harder.

Sarah: Without language, there would be no scientific knowledge. Humans have it, dogs don't.

Bob: Take knowledge humans and dogs both have. We and the dog all know there's water in his bowl.

Sarah: Not any more. He's finished it.

Bob: All right, we know there *was* water in his bowl. The dog doesn't have to prove it to anyone. He just knows. But you say *I* can't just know. I've got to prove it to any 'competent judge' who asks.

Sarah: You could always say 'I remember' when asked how you know.

Zac: It won't be enough, Sarah, if they ask you how you know you're not misremembering.

Bob: What can I say then, except that I *do* remember? Someone like you, Zac, would be better at making it up. You always have something to say.

Zac: You're right, Bob. I'm not the strong, silent type.

Bob: There's a man lives down my street. He can speak, but he's not very bright. If you asked him 'How do you know there was water in the dog's bowl?', the question would just throw him. He wouldn't even think to say 'I remember'. But he *would* remember. He'd still know, even though he couldn't give you a justification. It's not fair for intellectuals with the gift of the gab to set standards for knowing that suit them but exclude many of the rest of us.

Sarah: OK, but don't pretend his knowledge is part of science. Even if knowledge doesn't require proof, science sets a higher standard.

Bob: You said yourself, science is based on observation. Scientists rely on knowledge they get through their senses, like animals do.

Sarah: These days much of that is done by microscopes, telescopes, measuring instruments, which feed their results directly into computers, without human intervention. Experiments are repeated in other laboratories, results from different experiments are compared, statistical tests are applied. It's not like just looking out of the window and saying what you think you see.

Bob: Don't tell me there are no human technicians, looking after all those machines and making sure they work properly. *They* still rely on their eyes and ears.

Sarah: But still, the whole process is much more reliable than animal perception by itself.

Bob: Maybe. But when you learn from a science magazine, aren't you trusting your eyes to read, and the scientist who wrote it? Who says it's not a fraud?

Sarah: The article will have been checked by competent referees, other scientists, properly selected by the editor of the journal (not magazine, Bob).

Zac: Can't the editor choose lazy or biased referees, or pretend an article has been checked when it hasn't? You know as well as I do, Sarah, they're human too.

Sarah: Of course. Mistakes and frauds do happen, but in the long run they come to light and get corrected.

Bob: So you say, but I don't call it *proof*. Whatever we read in one science *journal* may get corrected in the next one. Even if it's false, there's no certainty it'll ever be corrected.

Sarah: You can't expect guarantees for much in this world, Bob.

Bob: You can for washing machines. Why not for science journals?

Sarah: You know I didn't mean that sort of guarantee, Bob. It doesn't stop the machine going wrong. We can only reduce unreliability, not eliminate it altogether. Fallibilism again.

Zac: Sarah, aren't you telling us to accept your scientific point of view on faith?

Sarah: No, I'm not. It's not like religion. Even with its glitches, science is the best means we have for producing knowledge of the world. That's totally different from a leap of faith, where you just plump for a point of view with no evidence of its truth. We agreed, knowing doesn't mean you can silence paranoid doubts.

Zac: So now you're diagnosing your opponents as mentally ill, Sarah? Isn't that how the Soviet Union used to deal with dissidents?

Bob: Are you saying I'm mad, Sarah?

Sarah: No, of course not. It's just Zac, trying to needle me.

Zac: The personality flaw is mine, is it, Sarah? Instead of taking seriously the argument I've been making about the inextricability of knowledge and power, you just denigrate those who don't accept your view. You're revealing the kind of treatment people can expect if they challenge the authority of science: psychiatric treatment.

Bob: Isn't that a bit of an exaggeration, Zac? I've never been persecuted for my belief in witchcraft, or locked up in a mental hospital, though I've had a few odd looks in my time.

Zac: With respect, Bob, you're not important enough. You're not exactly a threat to the scientific establishment. But we've had a hint of the methods they'll use when they *do* feel threatened.

Sarah: Isn't mockery more effective? It's easy to satirize opponents of science, flat-earthers, make them look ridiculous.

Zac: Yes, Sarah, satire is a powerful instrument of conservatism. Jokes depend on unexamined assumptions. Laughter is a substitute for thought.

Sarah: In my experience, satire usually attacks governments, not oppositions. If we don't ridicule the ridiculous, bad rulers will get away with even more. No one will laugh at their pompous rhetoric. A sense of humour is an antidote to tyranny.

Zac: Governments fall when they fail too blatantly to serve the values folk *already* have. What concerns me is the authority of those values themselves. That's where the hidden power lies. It belongs to the values people *don't* find funny. They laugh at judges whose sell-by date is long past; they don't laugh at *justice*.

Roxana: They laugh at truths, not truth.

Sarah: They laugh at rationality in practice, but not in principle.

Bob: Surely the reason people don't laugh at those values is that they're not funny.

Zac: No, Bob, they're not funny because people don't laugh at them.

Sarah: A mad dictator might laugh at truth and justice and even rationality.

Bob: If he did, he'd be *wrong*.

Zac: From whose point of view, Bob?

Bob: From that of all decent people.

Zac: Who decides who's decent, Bob?

Bob: Well, whether I'm decent or indecent, I don't laugh at truth or justice or rationality.

Sarah: Nor do I.

Roxana: Nor I. I have experienced their absence.

Zac: OK, all of you, silence me in the name of conservative values, like truth, justice, and rationality! You have the power. You outnumber me three to one.

I'll bet Roxana doesn't find logic funny, and Sarah doesn't find science funny.

Bob: Witchcraft is no laughing matter, either.

Roxana: Some proofs in logic are amusing.

Zac: Not for the rest of us, Roxana. This time I think I'm on the majority side.

Roxana: The loss is yours. You talk of knowledge and power. What political significance do you attribute to your chatter? I am not joking.

Zac: Liberation, Roxana, that's what it's all about. Such chatter, as you dismissively call it, helps us liberate ourselves from the silent domination of values imposed on us by invisible structures we never chose or felt. It alerts us to the hidden thought control over us, so we can rise up against it.

Sarah: In the name of what?

Bob: What are you liberating us to do?

Zac: Whatever you like, Bob.

Sarah: Doesn't what we like depend on what we value? Once you have freed us from our old values, what values do we have?

Zac: Whatever values you choose, Sarah.

Sarah: How does someone without values choose between values? At random?

Zac: Sarah, I'm not talking only about moral values. I'm talking about whole styles of thinking, forms of life, worldviews.

Sarah: That makes it even worse. How can someone with no way of thinking choose between ways of thinking—unthinkingly? Thinking at random would already be a way of thinking (a really bad one).

Bob: If you've no way of thinking, you must be brain dead.

Sarah: Zac, have you considered the *effect* of all your talk against hidden assumptions underlying rational argument? What it actually does is undermine the authority of rational argument.

Zac: What's so frightening about that, Sarah? You're a grown-up woman, you don't need a daddy to tell you what to do any more, not even a Big Daddy you call 'Rational Argument'.

Sarah: You leave my father out of this. I could just as easily accuse you of playing the naughty little boy, the spoilt son of over-indulgent parents who feels he can get away with anything and loves shocking visitors. The issue is your undermining of the authority of rational argument. What it liberates people to do is to act on their deepest prejudices, without having to justify them rationally. Don't assume that what they do then will be politically acceptable to you. If they feel liberated to choose injustice and cruelty, you may not like the results. You may be the first to be lined up against the wall and shot.

Zac: That's a danger any revolutionary thinker must live with, Sarah.

Bob: I spent a couple of years living in a commune when I was young. They said it was a liberated community and everyone's point of view was as good as everyone else's. The way it worked out, a few of them were the bosses.

Sarah: Were they all men?

Bob: Most of them. Bullies. They never hit anyone, they were just sure of themselves, smooth-tongued. They had the patter.

Sarah: How were decisions made?

Bob: Endless meetings. 'Free and open discussion'. If you spoke up against what they wanted, they talked you into the ground. Made you feel stupid. Officially we were all equal. But anyone could see who was on top. They slept with whoever they liked. If she resisted, they said she was in the grip of reactionary prejudices, and would be liberated from them. Sometimes it looked more like rape to me. If you tried to argue with them, they accused you of assuming your point of view was better than other people's. In the end, I got fed up with being liberated and left. Your ideas remind me of theirs, Zac.

Zac: That's so unfair, Bob.

Roxana: Zac appeals to the value of fairness.

Zac: I think *Bob* values fairness, Roxana.

Bob: I do. What do you mean, I was being unfair?

Zac: For a start, I'd never dream of raping anyone.

Roxana: A pity your waking thoughts are less disciplined than your sleeping ones.

Zac: I am deeply respectful of women, Roxana! One of my feminist friends told me I'm the most radical feminist she has ever met.

Bob: I didn't mean you're a rapist, Zac. How you talk just reminds me of how they talked, that's all.

Zac: What was their theoretical viewpoint, Bob?

Bob: They were always arguing about it. Theories, politics, hegemony, liberation, all that. I could hardly understand a word.

Sarah: It sounds like anarchism in theory, collective tyranny in practice.

Zac: I'm no anarchist, Sarah. My political position is totally different. It's far more complex and multi-layered. Anyway, whatever political position those guys claimed to be applying, we can't judge it by what happened in your commune, Bob. It's naïvely simple-minded to make so-called experience the test of theory.

Sarah: That's the scientific way to judge a theory, putting its predictions to the test of experience.

Zac: Sarah, don't forget, people may pretend to be applying political principles they don't actually care about, to make actions that suit them look legitimate. Or they may misunderstand the implications of their own theoretical point of view. Or an experiment may fail because people hostile to the theory interfere.

Sarah: Well, if we can't judge a political theory by experience, what's a better test?

Zac: You can rigorously analyse the theory itself, Sarah, to work out what its inner contradictions are, or whether it has liberating consequences. That's not imposing some external 'true' standard of rationality, it's just articulating the theory from within.

Sarah: Fine, but once you've articulated it, how do you judge whether what it's saying is *true*?

Zac: That word again, Sarah! I see myself and others like me as primarily *enablers*. We give people the intellectual tools to analyse their own circumstances and assumptions. What they do with those tools is up to them.

Bob: I get it. You're giving people bombs. What they throw them at is up to them.

Roxana: Fortunately, most of the bombs fail to go off.

Zac: They have time fuses, Roxana. They will go off sooner or later.

Roxana: That is what the manufacturers claim.

Zac: You just don't realize how explosive this sort of theorizing is, Roxana. It's far more relevant to the politics of today than most of what you see on the television news, and even more relevant to the politics of tomorrow.

Roxana: Its claim of political relevance is one more symptom of its political irrelevance.

Zac: You're thinking of the present political structure, Roxana—who gets how many votes and seats at the next election, that sort of thing. Intellectual revolutions take longer, but in the long run are far more radical.

Sarah: From a scientific point of view, there is far too *little* rational argument and use of evidence in politics, not too much. When you discourage respect for rational standards, Zac, the confusion you create is a smokescreen for politicians to hide behind, to avoid proper scrutiny, even though I'm sure you don't intend it that way. If I accuse a politician of falsehood and he replies that 'false' is a dangerous word, people *should* laugh. We'd be in trouble if instead their reaction was to nod with respect.

Zac: I'd love to live in a country with an openly relativist government, Sarah. It's not like the absolutist ones have such a great track record.

Sarah: Didn't you concede earlier that some relativists behave just like fallibilists?

Zac: Yes, Sarah. I can't speak for other relativists, but the sort of relativist government *I'd* favour would be much more tolerant of different cultures and different points of view.

Sarah: Just as fallibilists are tolerant. You must be certain you're right before you start persecuting others for being wrong.

Bob: For some people, persecuting is fun. They may not wait till they're certain.

Roxana: Will Zac's government discourage the use of the words 'true' and 'false' in public life? Will it permit their use in schools?

Zac: My government, as you call it, Roxana, would ask questions, not dictate answers.

Roxana: Asking questions is not governing. You do not want to govern, you want to criticize.

Zac: What's wrong with criticism, Roxana?

Roxana: Criticize all you like, but don't be surprised that someone else is taking the decisions.

Sarah: In science, criticizing theories is essential, but so is constructing them in the first place.

Bob: Why set them up, if it's only to knock them down?

Sarah: Not all get knocked down. Some are true. The theory that blood circulates is true: it does. And some false theories are near enough true to be useful approximations. Although Einstein refuted Newtonian physics, it's still used in the design of space rockets. Scientific theories get a defence as well as a prosecution. Otherwise, they would all be convicted without fair trial. And some of them are innocent.

Zac: 'Innocent' also means naïve. Criticism in science is always partial, Sarah. It never queries the deepest presuppositions of science itself.

Sarah: Such as?

Zac: Such as the very possibility of scientific language as a transparent medium through which to view the world.

Bob: What's Zac on about now?

Zac: I mean that science treats language as if it were a window on the world, Bob.

Bob: Does it? And isn't it?

Sarah: Scientists prefer just to get on with the science. They use language to describe the world, without wasting time asking philosophical questions about language itself.

Zac: Exactly, Sarah. They don't pause to reflect on what they're taking for granted.

Sarah: You haven't shown that science *does* presuppose that language is a window, or why it wouldn't be fine to do so.

Zac: And *you* haven't shown that it *doesn't*, or why it *would* be fine to do so.

Sarah: If science had to give further proof of everything it says, it could never get started.

Zac: Perhaps science as you imagine it never could get started, Sarah.

Sarah: Science as it really is *did* get started. It's good enough for me, warts and all.

Zac: Sarah, that's exactly the conservatism I'm complaining about. You don't question the way science is done, or what it claims for itself.

Sarah: I'm not saying science is perfect, but life is too short for an infinite sequence of questionings, and questionings of questionings, and questionings of questionings of questionings…One must start somewhere.

Roxana: Zac's questioning is selective too. Is that how he hopes to govern after all, by questioning what he dislikes and not questioning what he likes?

Sarah: A feared dictator could operate like that, always getting what he wanted while appearing never to dictate. His scared minions would destroy whatever he questioned, without being explicitly ordered to do so.

Bob: Who fears Zac?

Zac: This is my thanks! I try to act as a peacemaker between you, Sarah and Bob; I end up being abused by both sides. I ask a few questions, and get accused of trying to be a dictator.

Roxana: Peacemakers sometimes have their own agenda. Zac selects his questions strategically, not at random. Questioning truth but not liberation has different effects from questioning liberation but not truth.

Zac: I question *both*, Roxana.

Roxana: One line of questioning appears to be more urgent for you than the other.

Sarah: Whatever Zac is up to, can't we agree that we should be getting our disagreements out into the open, not muffling them up?

Zac: Sarah, the most effective way to get disagreement out into the open is *war*.

Sarah: Obviously I didn't mean that. I meant articulating the issues clearly and explicitly, removing any ambiguity or vagueness, in order to work out exactly what it is we disagree about.

Roxana: Diplomacy includes the art of using ambiguity and vagueness to construct forms of words on which all can agree, so all can save face.

Sarah: A last resort, if the only alternative is war. But we are not the statesmen of Europe in 1914. Once we have clarified the issues, we can start resolving them without killing each other. We can isolate the disagreements between us, identify the common ground we share, and use it as a starting point from which by rational argument we can find out who's right and who's wrong.

Roxana: Sometimes all are wrong.

Sarah: All the more reason to clarify the issues. Of course few theories are perfect. The process I'm describing often produces a theory better than any of those we started with. All of them may contribute to that end result.

Roxana: Why expect a happy ending? Why must it be possible to resolve all differences by rational argument?

Sarah: Suppose we disagree on the answer to a question. First we agree what evidence we have. Then we see which answer our evidence favours, and agree on that.

Roxana: Sometimes our evidence favours no answer.

Sarah: Then we agree to stay agnostic and open-minded while we gather more evidence. If we are really unlucky, we may have to remain agnostic forever. But usually in science, the evidence starts to accumulate in favour of one answer over the rest.

Roxana: And they all lived happily ever after.

Sarah: It's no fairy story, it's an idealization.

Bob: What's the difference?

Sarah: Scientists idealize all the time. In their calculations, physicists often treat planets as points with masses. Without such simplified models, the mathematics would be too hard even for a computer. The result can still be a very accurate prediction. Fairy stories don't make accurate predictions.

Roxana: What if the two sides cannot agree on what evidence they have?

Sarah: That's easy. If they can't agree to include something in their evidence, they agree to exclude it. We use only agreed evidence.

Bob: When I say I sensed the woman in black is a witch, you just object that it's not proper evidence. You give no reason, but it automatically gets excluded?

Sarah: I don't object to including 'Bob said he sensed the woman in black is a witch' in our evidence. We all heard you say that. But I'm not including 'Bob sensed the woman in black is a witch', because we don't agree that you sensed any such thing. You just *think* she's a witch.

Bob: If other people who knew about witchcraft were here, they'd have sensed it too.

Zac: You don't mind excluding other people's evidence, Sarah. How do you like it when someone else excludes *your* evidence?

Sarah: My evidence is scientifically verified. It can't be excluded.

Zac: Sceptics about man-made global warming will reject some of your scientific evidence, Sarah. They may claim scientists have fiddled the figures, or they may just reject it out of hand, giving no reason. According to you, it then gets excluded from the evidence, because it's not agreed.

Roxana: Soon no evidence of global warming will be left.

Bob: Phew, really hot today, for the time of year.

Zac: The sceptics may doubt even that, Bob.

Sarah: All right, my idealization went too far. They can't just reject evidence because it doesn't suit them. They must give a good reason for rejecting it.

Roxana: It is easy to invent something and call it a good reason.

Sarah: That's not enough. Something should be rejected as evidence only if both sides *agree* there's good reason to reject it.

Bob: I don't agree there's good reason to reject my sensing the woman's a witch.

Roxana: By her new criterion, Sarah cannot reject it as evidence.

Sarah: Oh dear, this is getting out of hand, isn't it? I'd better say something can be rejected as evidence if there *is* good reason to reject it, even if some crank on the other side doesn't agree.

Roxana: Then the evidence will not be agreed.

Sarah: The procedure may only work for reasonable people. I'm not sure what to do about the unreasonable ones. Education, I suppose.

Zac: What do you do if they don't want your education, Sarah? Imprison them so you can brainwash them?

Bob: Do I count as reasonable?

Sarah: Not about witchcraft. You do about gardening.

Roxana: Why do you expect *reasonable* people to agree on their evidence?

Sarah: If two people can't agree on their shared evidence, at least one of them is being unreasonable.

Roxana: Which one?

Zac: The one who disagrees with Sarah, of course, Roxana.

Sarah: I think you're all being rather unfair. I was only offering an idealized model of a rational process for reaching agreement. I readily conceded that. Of course reality will be much less neat and tidy. But if we can manage even a rough approximation to the model, that's still progress worth making.

Zac: Sarah, how do you 'manage' progress, as you put it? How do you make people move toward your model, not away from it? Won't you need force for crowd control, to police progress? You'll be using batons on those who head off in unauthorized directions.

Sarah: You talk as if humans had no natural tendency in the direction I'm describing, and rational discussion were something quite alien to us. If we're really like that, perhaps my model is hopeless. But I'm less pessimistic. If a group of humans find themselves with a down-to-earth practical problem to solve, they usually discuss it reasonably, and agree a sensible solution.

Zac: What about all the times when, for some of them, religious or moral or magical prohibitions forbid what you would call the obvious solution, Sarah? Things can get heated then, especially if others reject that religious or moral or magical point of view.

Sarah: If they'd been better educated, they wouldn't have had those religious or moral or magical prejudices in the first place.

Zac: Who will appoint you Minister for Education, Sarah?

Sarah: A politician is the last thing I want to be.

Zac: Then you don't get to appoint someone else as Minister for Education either, Sarah. You can't wash your hands of power and still expect to get what you want.

Roxana: As King Lear discovered.

Sarah: Well, I have a vote. Unfortunately mine alone doesn't make much difference. I just have to hope other people agree with me.

Bob: Do they?

Sarah: Far fewer than I'd like, alas.

Bob: If it's any consolation, Ministers for Education don't control what ordinary people think.

Zac: Why do you say that, Bob? In many countries they control what goes into school textbooks.

Bob: My problem at school was, what went into our textbooks wouldn't go into my head. Even when it did, it didn't stay there long.

Sarah: I'm sure your belief in witchcraft didn't come from school. Where *did* it come from, Bob?

Bob: My granny often looked after me when I was a kid. She kept talking about witches. She thought one of her neighbours was one. She was probably right. I was really scared whenever I had to walk past that neighbour's house alone. Sometimes I caught that woman looking out of the window at me. Later, as a teenager, I didn't take witchcraft seriously. I started thinking about it again as I grew older. The more I think about it, the more it makes sense. I met other people with experience of witchcraft too. So much happens that can be explained no other way. My whole life is evidence for witchcraft.

Sarah: What an unscientific attitude!

Roxana: Bob accepts the witchcraft theory on the grounds that it explains his evidence better than other theories do. He makes an inference to the best explanation. Is that an unscientific method?

Sarah: Of course inference to the best explanation is a scientific method, but Bob is hopelessly misapplying it. Witchcraft isn't really the best explanation of his data. However, I can see I'm never going to change your mind, Bob.

Bob: I can see *I'm* never going to change *your* mind about witches, Sarah.

Sarah: If the evidence supports it, I'll gladly accept witchcraft. That's the scientific attitude.

Bob: Whatever experiences I gave you, they wouldn't change your mind. If I told you I'd seen witches flying through the air on broomsticks, you'd just accuse me of lying, or misremembering, or misinterpreting.

Sarah: Well, you would be.

Bob: You didn't even bother to ask if I *have* seen witches on broomsticks.

Sarah: Have you?

Bob: No, but a friend of a friend of mine has. He's well known for his honesty.

Sarah: He may be sincere, but he isn't truthful.

Zac: It's dialectical deadlock between you two, Sarah and Bob, as I said when I first introduced myself. Neither of you will ever change the other's mind. That's why you need a new attitude for peaceful co-existence.

Bob: What new attitude?

Zac: For a start, Bob, each of you should acknowledge that the other is right from their point of view.

Sarah: We've heard that before. It just means acknowledging that the other *thinks* they're right. I didn't need your help to realize that Bob thinks he's right, and he didn't need it to realize that I think I'm right.

Zac: More than that, Sarah. The two of you should agree that each of you can make sense of things in your own way.

Sarah: No! Bob *doesn't* make sense of things. When one examines his ideas in detail, one sees that they *don't* properly explain anything much. They don't provide serious predictions. They are just bits and pieces he makes up as he goes along.

Bob: They're not! I can't give you equations like scientists can. I was never much good at maths in school. Much cleverer people than me study how witch-craft works. The more advanced witches know.

Zac: From Bob's point of view, witchcraft makes sense of things. From Sarah's point of view, modern science makes sense of things.

Sarah: That just means that Bob *thinks* that witchcraft makes sense of things, and I think that modern science makes sense of things. We didn't need your help to realize that either.

Roxana: Bob and Sarah are in conflict because their beliefs are incompatible. If they just add more beliefs, on Zac's advice or not, the original incompatibility will remain. The only way to remove it is by subtracting beliefs from Bob or Sarah or both.

Bob: No one's taking away any of my beliefs about witchcraft.

Sarah: And I'm not giving up any of my scientific beliefs.

Zac: I'm not asking either of you to give up any of your beliefs! I'm trying to *respect* both points of view, not *destroy* them.

Sarah: I'm not dogmatic in my beliefs.

Bob: That's what you think.

Sarah: I revise them when the evidence warrants it. But I don't need your funny theories, Zac, to change my mind.

Zac: Without my 'funny theories', Sarah, what framework have you and Bob for discussing witchcraft without coming to blows?

Bob: I'd never hit a woman.

Sarah: Science uses rational methods, not violence.

Zac: I didn't mean *literal* blows, in your case. Excluding another's point of view is itself a form of violence, one of the most insidious forms.

Sarah: When you first interrupted our argument, we were about three minutes from agreeing to disagree. What better outcome are you offering?

Roxana: He gave you something else to argue about, and someone else to argue with.

Sarah: Thank you for that, Zac; I enjoy a good argument. I'd hate living in a world without disagreement. So boring!

Bob: I wouldn't mind.

Zac: At least I warned you of the danger of intolerance in thinking in terms of true and false, right and wrong.

Sarah: What I learned was the danger of doublethink in trying *not* to think in those terms.

Bob: I think I got from Roxana, the logical way of using them is just common sense, handled with care.

Sarah: I discovered that fallibilism isn't as straightforward as I thought. Juggling fallibility and knowledge, it's hard to keep them both in the air for long. But we must.

Bob: I'll say this for Zac. He confirmed my suspicion that science is less different from politics than scientists pretend. Knowledge is all mixed up with power. But that doesn't mean it's nothing more than power.

Zac: Well, Bob, at least you got *something* out of what I was saying. But you and Sarah still haven't resolved your original deadlock over witchcraft. I offered you an escape route, which both of you refused.

Roxana: Because it led nowhere. They cannot agree. It is pointless to pretend otherwise.

Sarah: We can live happily with our disagreement.

Bob: I'd rather we agreed.

Zac: So how do *you* interpret their deadlock, Roxana?

Roxana: Either witchcraft works or it does not. On that, either Bob is right and Sarah is wrong, or Sarah is right and Bob is wrong. I know which without caring which. I have no special interest in the question of witchcraft. I listen to their dispute merely as an instructive example of the chaotic nature of debate between untrained persons. By the normal rules of informal argument, neither of them secured a decisive advantage.

Zac: You see? That's just what I was saying, Roxana.

Roxana: You did even worse than either of them, Zac, when arguing for your views, or trying to defend them, because you kept shifting your ground without admitting it.

Zac: It's called flexibility, Roxana.

Roxana: No, it is called 'muddle'. In any case, the normal rules of informal argument allow any determined player of average intelligence to remain undefeated indefinitely, by continually calling into question their opponent's claims. It is not an interesting test.

Zac: Then what is an interesting test, Roxana?

Roxana: Outside pure logic and mathematics, the interesting tests are all far harder to referee. They include the test: which theory best explains the evidence? Both Bob and Sarah attempted to apply that test, though in a primitive manner, and with conflicting results.

Zac: Roxana, you're saying it was a draw.

Roxana: I am not. I am saying that it takes a good judge to decide who won. Whichever side is declared the winner, the other will predictably accuse the judge of bias. Zac wants to be liked by both sides, so he is afraid to declare a winner, even to himself. As a result, neither side likes him. Neither regards him as a friend.

Sarah: I don't dislike you, Zac.

Bob: Nor do I.

Zac: It was a draw. At least neither of you, Sarah and Bob, will hate me for saying that. What about you, Roxana? Will you declare a result?

Roxana: No. Like Zac, I will not declare a winner. Unlike him, I will also not declare it a draw.

Zac: Why not, Roxana?

Roxana: Their performances were probably unequal in merit. Neither of them did very well. I lack appetite for the task of estimating which of them did worse. Not only are the standards for comparing explanations messy and vague, it is unclear exactly what evidence there is to be explained. I prefer to solve more precisely defined problems.

Zac: You don't care whether people like *you*, do you, Roxana?

Roxana: No. If I cared, I might become confused, like you. I do not even care whether I like myself. I prefer to take a purely logical point of view.

Sarah: Despite all your crazy anti-scientific ideas, Bob, I can't help liking you.

Bob: And I can't help liking you, Sarah, despite your narrow-minded worship of conventional science.

Zac: That's wonderful, Bob and Sarah. Please don't think I feel left out. I'm not done yet.

{ PART IV }

The Vices of Value

Sarah: Did you see that woman? The one in lurid pink. She slapped her little boy, quite hard, just because he was crying. I've a good mind to report her. Look! She's done it again.

Bob: My mum often slapped me, when I got too much for her. It never did me any harm. I preferred being slapped to when she was angry with me in a cold, silent way.

Zac: Times have changed, Bob.

Sarah: It's *outrageous* to use violence on a child. The social services should intervene.

Bob: And take her son into care?

Sarah: If necessary.

Bob: That would be much worse for him than being looked after by his own mum and getting a few slaps.

Sarah: How can you be so complacent, Bob? That child is being physically and psychologically hurt in front our eyes.

Bob: He looks happy enough now, playing.

Sarah: You have no idea of the long-term effects. That child may be damaged for life.

Bob: Like me?

Sarah: You might not have needed to take refuge in absurd superstitions if your mother hadn't abused you.

Bob: It wasn't abuse, just slapping.

Sarah: Slapping is abuse, Bob. If I slapped you right now, which I almost feel like doing just to make you see sense, I could be prosecuted for assault. Defenceless children deserve to be protected *at least* as much as adults are by law, *especially* when their attackers are the very people who are supposed to be protecting them.

Bob: You keep saying we must be scientific about everything. What's the scientific evidence for your ideas about slapping, then?

Sarah: I'm sure there's plenty of statistical evidence for the damaging long-term effects of hitting children.

Bob: You mean you don't know of any, you're just sure there is some. Anyway, parents have the right to bring up their children as they see fit. They know best what their children need.

Sarah: Not always. That woman clearly doesn't. Some parents *kill* their own children. Is that knowing best what they need?

Bob: Killing a child isn't bringing it up. Anyway, I wasn't talking about *mad* parents. I meant *normal* parents. That woman down the carriage isn't mad, just tired and fed up, with a whining brat to look after all the time. Normal parents have the right to bring up their children as they see fit.

Sarah: Even if their methods are scientifically proven to harm children?

Bob: It's not some scientist's right to decide how that boy should be looked after. It's his *mum's* right. Whether she brings him up on scientific advice is up to her. Sometimes a good old-fashioned cuff round the ear is just what a boy needs.

Sarah: I don't believe she has any idea what the scientific advice is.

Bob: Well, go and tell her then, if you're so worked up about it.

Sarah: I will do exactly that. Someone needs to take some action.

Zac: Are you sure that's wise, Sarah?...Too late.

Bob: I didn't think she'd take what I said seriously. She puts her money where her mouth is, our action woman Sarah. She's talking to that woman now. It's so noisy, I can't hear what they're saying. Can you, Zac?

Zac: No, I can't. Bob, perhaps you should be more careful about provoking Sarah.

Bob: I know, she takes everything so seriously. I can't quite see what's happening....Ah, she's coming back. What did she say, Sarah?

Sarah: I could only make out half her words. Most of those were obscenities I'd rather not repeat.

Bob: Did her boy say anything?

Sarah: He started to cry again. Then she threatened to set the police on *me*, for upsetting him—I could make that much out. There was no point continuing.

Bob: There was no point starting.

Sarah: The whole incident simply confirms my suspicion. The child should be taken into care.

Bob: Is that what science tells you, or are you just cross with her for swearing at you?

Sarah: You're right, I must be careful not to lose my objectivity. But I objected to her slapping him even before I went and talked to her.

Bob: She had a moral right to slap him, whatever the law says. None of your science can prove otherwise.

Sarah: It can prove the damaging long-term effects of parental violence on the health and happiness of children.

Bob: I'm talking about a mother's right. She has the right to use her own judgement in bringing up her child.

Sarah: Not when her own judgement manifests so much ignorance and stupidity.

Bob: She had a right to slap him!

Sarah: You're wrong, she had no right!

Zac: Bob and Sarah, this is where I came in. You're deadlocked again.

Roxana: What does Sarah's science say about moral rights?

Sarah: Well, 'moral right' isn't a scientific term. You can't measure moral rights. But you *can* measure health, and even happiness. It would be more scientific to talk about them.

Bob: Don't change the subject. I'm talking about a mother's moral rights.

Sarah: That sort of emotive language gets us nowhere. To make progress in discussing children's upbringing, we need to start using more factual vocabulary.

Bob: It's a fact that a mother has a moral right to slap her child.

Sarah: Moral rights aren't facts, they are matters of opinion. Matters of fact are the sort of thing that can be measured scientifically.

Roxana: Once scientists have made all their measurements, how do they decide what ought to be done?

Sarah: They recommend the option that maximizes probable health and happiness.

Roxana: They assume the moral theory that we ought to maximize probable health and happiness?

Sarah: What's the alternative?

Roxana: There are infinitely many.

Zac: Sarah, health and happiness are not the only things a moral theory might say you ought to maximize. Some people say you ought to maximize total pleasure minus total pain.

Sarah: Don't they come to the same thing?

Zac: They needn't, Sarah. You might maximize total pleasure minus total pain by making everyone take a pill that gave them ten seconds of unimaginably intense pleasure and then instant death—like sex, only more so. That pill isn't the healthy item on the menu.

Sarah: Not with those after-effects. I don't think it's even what I meant by happiness. I had something more long term in mind.

Bob: I don't know about maximizing anything. What's that to do with a mother's right to bring up her child as she sees fit?

Roxana: There is nothing scientific about Sarah's scientists' choice of moral theory.

Sarah: I wasn't thinking clearly enough. To choose a moral theory is to make a value judgement, and science doesn't make value judgements. Choosing a morality is ultimately just a matter of individual preference.

Roxana: Like choosing the colour of your bedroom walls?

Sarah: Well, my morality affects more people than the colour of my bedroom walls.

Bob: Can I choose my own morality, because it is just my preference?

Sarah: You choose your morality, and I'll choose mine. But mine tells me to prevent some of the effects of yours, by not letting parents strike their children.

Bob: Your morality tries to thwart mine, but you're not saying yours is right and mine is wrong?

Sarah: Yours is right relative to your preferences. Mine is right relative to my preferences. No morality is absolutely true or absolutely false.

Zac: So you are a relativist after all, Sarah. I knew you'd catch on eventually.

Roxana: Catching a disease is not catching on.

Sarah: I'm not Zac (and I don't like your metaphors as much as he does). I'm no relativist about science. Some scientific theories are absolutely true, others are absolutely false. By scientific method, we find out which are which. But that method doesn't apply to moral values. You can't observe or measure them. They are invented qualities, not discovered quantities. That's why I'm a relativist just about morality, a moral relativist.

Bob: I can't keep up with all your changes of mind, Sarah. The last I heard, you and Roxana thought Zac's relativism was full of holes. Won't there be the same holes in your new moral relativism?

Sarah: Fair question. But there's a crucial difference. Zac wants to be a relativist about *everything*. That's why we could never pin him down.

Zac: I'm no dead butterfly, Sarah.

Roxana: A live butterfly, with a butterfly mind.

Sarah: *Whatever* Zac said, he then relativized to his point of view. He even had to be a relativist about his own relativism. That's why he got into trouble.

Zac: I wasn't troubled, Sarah.

Roxana: That was part of your trouble.

Sarah: My moral relativism only concerns moral beliefs, beliefs about what we ought to do. Moral relativism doesn't tell you what you ought to do, so I needn't be relativist about it. Moral relativism is *absolutely* true, not just true for me. It's true whatever anyone thinks. It's limited enough to be defensible, unlike Zac's.

Zac: 'Limited' is the word.

Roxana: After her change of mind, does Sarah still maintain that what ought to be done is what maximizes health and happiness?

Sarah: Of course. I haven't changed my morals during this conversation. I still deplore slapping children. I just had to remind myself how different morals are from science.

Roxana: But you still think that health and happiness can be measured scientifically?

Sarah: Absolutely, in principle.

Roxana: So the quantity your moral theory says we ought to maximize can be measured scientifically.

Sarah: Yes, that's one of the advantages of a moral theory like mine.

Roxana: Then why did you deny that moral qualities can be measured?

Sarah: Oh, I see what you mean. But the measurements are relative to my moral theory.

Roxana: You mean that their accuracy as measurements of what ought to be maximized depends on your theory?

Sarah: I suppose so.

Roxana: All science is like that. When you measure temperature with an ordinary thermometer, its accuracy depends on a theory about the behaviour of mercury. You accept the theory about mercury, so you accept that temperature can be measured by a thermometer.

Sarah: I do think, on my own behalf, that one can measure what ought to be done. But that's all relative to my point of view.

Zac: Go, Sarah!

Sarah: I'd feel more confident without your support.

Roxana: Before, you based your moral relativism on the unmeasurability of moral qualities. Now you say that they can be measured, but you still maintain your moral relativism.

Sarah: I'm not putting this very well. The difference is that we can agree answers to scientific questions, while we can't to moral questions. You saw the deadlock between Bob and me on the morality of hitting children.

Zac: Sarah, I also saw the deadlock between you and Bob on what caused his wall to collapse. That's a scientific question, in your sense, not a moral one.

Sarah: That time Bob was being unreasonable about witchcraft.

Roxana: But this time he is being reasonable about hitting children?

Sarah: No, he's being totally unreasonable about it! From my point of view. From *his* point of view, he's being totally reasonable about hitting children.

Bob: Quite right.

Roxana: From Bob's point of view, he was also being totally reasonable about witchcraft.

Bob: Quite right too.

Sarah: I suppose so, from your point of view. But in the case of witchcraft, your point of view is just plain wrong. In the case of hitting children, it's a matter of opinion.

Roxana: You assume the difference for which you were supposed to argue.

Sarah: Look, even if it's hard to be totally precise about it, isn't it obvious to everyone that scientific statements can be tested in a way moral statements can't?

Zac: It's not obvious to me, Sarah. All testing depends on a point of view.

Sarah: Well, the difference is obvious to *me*, Zac. As a result, I describe scientific statements as true or false. I don't describe moral statements as true or false.

Roxana: But you still *make* moral statements? You still say that hitting children is wrong?

Sarah: Yes. Hitting children *is* wrong.

Roxana: Yet, given what you said seconds ago, you will not describe that moral statement as true?

Sarah: No. It isn't *true* that hitting children is wrong.

Bob: Make up your mind, Sarah. First you say something, then you say that what you just said isn't true.

Roxana: Sarah has violated the elementary logic of truth again.

Sarah: OK, it is true that hitting children is wrong. From my point of view, not from Bob's.

Bob: Now you're being as slippery as Zac was.

Zac: Better slippery than simplistic, Bob.

Bob: Sarah, if you think something's true, can't you just come out and say it's true, without qualifying it like a dodgy lawyer?

Sarah: OK, Bob, if you insist. It's true that hitting children is wrong.

Roxana: Sarah describes moral statements as true or false after all.

Sarah: This relativism about morals isn't doing much better than Zac's about everything. Just limiting it to morals doesn't plug all the holes.

Zac: Sarah, maybe it's not clever to start with the big stuff, like morals. It may be better to start small and work up.

Sarah: How do you mean?

Zac: Take something that doesn't matter much, like etiquette, Sarah.

Bob: I was brought up to hold good manners very important. I must admit, though, I was often cheeky as a boy.

Zac: But manners aren't a matter of life and death, like morality, are they, Bob?

Bob: They can be. These days people get gunned down in the street for showing disrespect to a gang leader.

Sarah: But that's a disproportionate reaction. It bears out Zac's point: violating a rule of morality by murdering someone is far worse than violating a rule of etiquette by being disrespectful.

Zac: Thank you, Sarah. Take burping, for example. In some countries, it's polite to burp after a meal. Here, it's rude. Who thinks their rule is absolutely better or worse than ours?

Roxana: My brother used to burp after meals. It was culturally accepted, but I found it disgusting.

Bob: My cousin thinks not burping after a meal is stiff and pompous.

Zac: Those reactions cancel each other out, OK, everyone? Cultures are complicated, but just for argument's sake pretend it's simple: there are burping cultures and non-burping cultures. Burping after a meal is rude for a non-burping culture and polite for a burping culture. It's not rude or polite *absolutely*. We're all relativists about a case like that. We can use it as a template to work out how to be relativists about harder cases, like morals.

Roxana: It matters who burps, and in what circumstances.

Sarah: Obviously. If I burp after a meal on this train in this country, that's rude. If Roxana's brother burps after a meal at his home in his country, that's polite. I'm less sure about his burping on this train, or my burping in his house.

Roxana: He would laugh. Ignore him. Sarah does not make the politeness of a burp relative to who describes it. She makes it depend on the burper and the circumstances of the burping.

Zac: What's the difference, Roxana?

Sarah: *If* I thought Roxana's brother was rude to burp in his own home, I'd just be wrong, through ignorance of his culture. *His* burps in *his* home aren't just polite for his culture and rude for mine. They are just polite. His culture is the one that counts for them, since they happened within it.

Bob: Buuuuuuuuuurp. Buurp.

Sarah: Bob, really!

Bob: Sorry, I couldn't resist giving you an example to discuss.

Sarah: Thanks. If Roxana's brother were here, he might regard Bob's burps as polite.

Roxana: He would.

Sarah: But he'd just be wrong, through ignorance of our culture.

Roxana: Through contempt for it.

Sarah: Anyway, Bob's burps weren't just polite for his culture and rude for mine—and Bob's. They were just rude. Our culture is the one that counts, since they happened within it.

Roxana: Relativism fails to provide a culturally sensitive classification of burps.

Zac: Turning away from individual burps for a moment, Roxana, we are still relativists about generalizations like 'Burping is rude' and 'Burping is polite'.

Sarah: No, both generalizations are just false. Roxana's brother's burps are counterexamples to 'Burping is rude'. Bob's burps are counterexamples to 'Burping is polite'.

Zac: Sarah, you are interpreting people who say such things as generalizing over all cultures. Perhaps they mean to talk only about their own culture. So if you say 'Burping is rude' and Roxana's brother says 'Burping is polite', each of you speaks truly about your own culture.

Roxana: That is not relativism. It is just an instance of the commonplace phenomenon that what a sentence expresses depends on the context in which it is uttered. In effect, Sarah says 'Burping in my culture is rude' and my brother says 'Burping in my culture is polite'. Their statements are consistent, just as when Sarah says 'I am a woman' and my brother says 'I am not a woman'. Once the statements are clarified, it is clear to both cultures that both Sarah and my brother spoke truly.

Sarah: It's like legality. Slapping children is legal in some countries and illegal in others. Whether a slap is legal depends on where it happened. You can't legalize or illegalize slaps outside your own jurisdiction. Relativity to a point of view doesn't come into it.

Roxana: Zac misjudged in taking etiquette as an easy case for relativism.

Sarah: Morals are different. Each culture gets to settle which acts within it are polite or rude, but not to settle which acts within it are morally right or wrong. Even if everyone in another society thinks slavery is right—even the slaves themselves may think so—that doesn't settle the question for us. We still condemn *their* institution of slavery as wrong.

Roxana: Is Sarah still a relativist about the condemnation?

Sarah: Yes. I see no scientific basis for anything else. I admit, though, I can't see exactly how moral relativism would work.

Roxana: Would you support outside intervention to free the slaves?

Sarah: Yes, slavery is intolerable.

Roxana: If you had to justify the intervention to the slaveholders, what would you say?

Sarah: I'd talk about the suffering of the slaves, and try to get the slaveholders to see things from their point of view.

Roxana: The slaveholders hear that you are a moral relativist. They ask you whether your condemnation of slavery is any better absolutely than their defence of slavery. How do you reply?

Sarah: Coming out right then as a relativist might not be a very smart move politically, I see that. But I wouldn't want to be dishonest with them, either. If I couldn't persuade them to give up slaveholding voluntarily, I suppose I'd only be intervening if I had superior military force. I'd tell them I was intervening militarily because they wouldn't see reason.

Zac: How is switching their point of view for yours 'seeing reason', Sarah, if yours is no better absolutely than theirs?

Sarah: I could just tell them I had the power to free the slaves and was going to use it.

Bob: Brute force, eh?

Zac: If the balance of power shifted, Sarah, they might just tell you they had the power to enslave you and were going to use it.

Sarah: Maybe it doesn't matter *what* I tell the slaveholders. There's probably nothing I can say that would ever change their minds. The slaves shouldn't have to wait in chains for the miracle of my finding an argument that convinces the slaveholders against all their prejudices.

Roxana: Even if you cannot justify intervening in a way that convinces the slaveholders, you might wish to justify it in a way that convinced *you*.

Sarah: True. To feel justified in taking military action, I'd need to think that freeing the slaves was better than doing nothing about it—absolutely better, not just better from my own point of view. That's not what a moral relativist should say, though, is it?

Zac: OK, since you all made such a fuss about etiquette, let's try a different toy example to show how relativism works. Take the distinction between *interesting* and *boring*. It really matters to us. We want to spend our time doing interesting stuff, not boring stuff. We want to meet interesting people (like you three), not boring ones. But what's boring is relative to who you are. Roxana, what you say would bore many people, though of course it interests me.

Roxana: According to your Nietzsche, the truth has fewest defenders not when it is dangerous but when it is boring. I prefer boring truths to interesting falsehoods.

Sarah: I can't justify military intervention on the grounds that intervening bores me less than not intervening.

Zac: I know, Sarah, I know. I'm putting all the extra complications of morality to one side for now, in order to start with a simpler case. My point is this. If something interests me, I can say 'It's interesting'. If it bores others, they can say 'It's boring'. It's interesting for me, boring for them. That's all. It's senseless to ask whether it's interesting or boring *absolutely*.

Roxana: If something bores someone, and he calls it 'boring', can he be wrong?

Zac: How could he be, Roxana? The boring is simply whatever bores you.

Roxana: Even if it bores him only because he pays it insufficient attention?

Zac: It's still boring for *him*, Roxana. If I pay it more attention and so it doesn't bore me, then it isn't boring for *me*.

Sarah: Imagine you write a book, Zac, full of fascinating material.

Zac: I like the example, Sarah.

Sarah: I thought you would, Zac, at least that part, but it turns sour. A newspaper gets a journalist to review your book. Unfortunately, he's a lazy hack, with a low boredom threshold. He just flicks through your book, too superficially to get drawn in. He writes in his review 'Zac's book is boring'. Isn't his statement false?

Zac: I wouldn't say *false*, Sarah, so much as misleading. It would have been more honest and open if he'd said 'Zac's book bored me, but it may interest other readers'.

Roxana: Statements about what bored whom are irrelevant, because they do not raise the issue of relativism. Your book *did* bore the journalist; anyone who thinks otherwise is just mistaken. It is calling the book interesting or boring, without specifying *for whom*, that raises the issue of relativism.

Sarah: Surely the purpose of a book review isn't just to express the reviewer's idiosyncratic reaction to the book. It's to tell potential readers what the book is like, so they can make an informed choice whether to splash out money buying it. Whether it bored the reviewer matters mainly as evidence of whether it would bore readers of the review. In the review, the words 'boring' and 'interesting' should mean what would bore or interest readers of the review, not what bored or interested the reviewer.

Zac: Fair point, Sarah. When such words are spoken, hearers' reactions count, as well as the speaker's. But my point still holds, because audiences, even potential audiences, differ. A talk on accountancy may interest an audience of accountants and bore an audience of soccer fans.

Bob: I've met several accountants at soccer matches.

Zac: Yes, Bob, but most soccer fans aren't accountants. I'm talking general tendencies. Take some accountants who aren't soccer fans, and some soccer fans who aren't accountants. The accountants agree the talk was interesting, the soccer fans agree it was boring. The two sides disagree, in a sense, even though neither is at fault. That's where relativism comes in.

Sarah: It doesn't sound like genuine disagreement to me. The accountants just mean 'The talk was interesting *for accountants*'. The soccer fans just mean 'It was boring *for soccer fans*'. There's no disagreement there.

Zac: They might not realize the need for such qualifications, Sarah.

Sarah: Well, if the accountants mean 'The talk was interesting *for everyone*', they are plain wrong. And if the soccer fans mean 'It was boring for everyone', they are plain wrong too. Then both sides are at fault.

Bob: If the accountants are like the ones I met, they'll think everyone *ought* to find the talk interesting. They'll blame the other soccer fans' boredom on their stupidity and ignorance. And if the soccer fans are like some I've met, they'll think everyone ought to find the talk boring. They'll blame the accountants' interest on their drab personalities.

Roxana: The interesting is not what interests but what *should* interest. The boring is not what bores but what *should* bore.

Sarah: If that's what the two sides mean, they disagree about how everyone should react to the talk. I still say both sides are at fault. The accountants are wrong because the soccer fans aren't obliged to find the talk interesting. The soccer fans are wrong because the accountants aren't obliged to find it boring.

Roxana: Where has Sarah's relativism about obligation gone?

Sarah: Following Zac, I'm putting it to one side.

Roxana: With relief.

Bob: Everyone should be interested in witchcraft. It's too dangerous not to be.

Sarah: No, it's science, not witchcraft, that's worthy of everyone's interest. Even if science bored everyone in the whole world, that would just show what incurious minds they had. Science would still be really interesting, even if nobody recognized the fact.

Zac: What is this idea of the interesting-in-itself that doesn't interest any real people, Sarah? Anyway, if we treat 'interesting' and 'boring' as value terms, they'll be way too complex to be helpful models of relativism. Let's keep it simple, and treat the interesting as what interests and the boring as what bores.

Sarah: Interests or bores *whom*?

Zac: That depends on the context, Sarah, where the words are used.

Sarah: So in an accountancy context, 'interesting' and 'boring' mean what interests or bores accountants. In a soccer context, they mean what interests or bores soccer fans?

Zac: Let's run with that, Sarah.

Sarah: We've been there before. If the talk is called 'interesting' in an accountancy context and 'boring' in a soccer context, there's no fault but also no dis-agreement. It's just verbal.

Zac: What if an accountant calls it 'interesting' and a soc-cer fan calls it 'boring' in a *shared* context, Sarah?

Sarah: From what you said, in the shared context there is a comparison class, of people whose reactions count—maybe all accountants and all soccer fans, maybe just accountants who are also soccer fans, whatever.

Zac: OK, Sarah.

Sarah: So the accountant is wrong unless the talk would interest the people in the comparison class, and the soccer fan is wrong unless it would bore them. But it can't do both. So either the accountant or the soccer fan is wrong. Someone is at fault.

Zac: But who, Sarah?

Sarah: It doesn't really matter, Zac. Whoever is at fault, it isn't the faultless disagreement you seem to want. In real life we could probably find out who was wrong, by sampling audience reactions. If the reactions were too mixed, maybe both sides would be wrong. Your attempts to find a simple working model of relativism haven't gone very well, have they?

Roxana: The thin end of Zac's wedge keeps breaking.

Zac: I went too far playing your game, Roxana. I tried to keep it clear and simple. The lesson is that it's *never* clear and simple. It's always obscure and compli-cated. We acknowledge that by aspiring towards relativism, even though it always eludes a clear, simple statement. That's a sign of its adequacy to life. Clear, simple ideas are the traps.

Sarah: Any old drivel can be defended like that. It's a counsel of despair. Science shows how simple laws can explain complex phenomena. We'll probably never achieve perfect clarity and simplicity, but that doesn't mean we shouldn't try to get as close as we can.

Zac: You're still assuming that the closer we get, the better, Sarah. I'm challenging that. Sometimes we understand more deeply by getting *more* obscure and *more* complicated.

Roxana: Those with a taste for obscurity and complication can always convince themselves that they understand more deeply.

Sarah: Science recognizes that the world is full of obscurities and complications. It respects them, by insisting that we observe them carefully and describe them exactly, as a first step to identifying and explaining the underlying patterns. That does them far more justice than just discussing them in obscure and complicated ways. *You* chose the examples, Zac. You couldn't refute clear, simple ways of understanding them that avoided relativism.

Zac: But what about you, Sarah? Where are you coming from now? Before, you relativized moral questions, because they can't be settled scientifically. Now you speak of relativism like something the cat brought in.

Sarah: I'm not sure, to be honest. Even local relativisms don't look promising to me now, but nor does anything else. When I think of science, I can't take moral talk seriously, as a description of reality, but I can't avoid it when I think of that woman slapping her little boy. At least I don't pretend my muddle is the solution to the problem.

Zac: Sarah, your 'muddle' may not be a 'solution' in your sense, but it's how you can live with the problem. Why not take moral discourse seriously but not as a *description of reality*? It's not meant to be that. It's meant to be a way of *changing* reality instead. What use is morality if it's all talk and no action? 'Slapping children is wrong' is meant to *stop* people slapping children.

Sarah: That's not good enough for me. If I hadn't thought I was just right, and the mother just wrong, I wouldn't have felt entitled to go and stop her.

Bob: Much good it did.

Sarah: At least I tried.

Zac: Didn't you insist earlier that relativism doesn't imply tolerance, Sarah?

Sarah: I'm not talking about what some confused philosophical theory may or may not imply. I intervened because I thought I knew she was wrong to slap him, just as I thought I knew she *had* slapped him. If what I thought I knew is an illusion, that undermines my reason for acting.

Zac: So now you want moral knowledge as well as moral truth, Sarah?

Sarah: Yes, but I'm pulled both ways. I have no idea how anyone could possibly know right from wrong. But if 'Slapping children is wrong' is just an order to stop slapping children, what authority does it have? Why should anyone obey?

Zac: You are the one giving this order, Sarah.

Sarah: Yes, but saying that I was only obeying orders isn't suddenly a better excuse when I was the one who gave the orders.

Zac: Sarah, telling someone not to slap her son can't be compared to what concentration camp guards did.

Sarah: Obviously not. Normally I'd say we know full well the moral difference. But once I start doubting that we have moral knowledge, I feel lost. Nothing looks like an adequate justification for intervening in the lives of others, against their wishes.

Roxana: Why do you regard moral knowledge as hard to obtain?

Sarah: Just think about it. There's such a difference between knowing the slap happened and knowing it was wrong. The slap was a physical event. By the normal process of vision, it caused various effects in my brain, which meant I saw it and knew it had occurred. The wrongness of the slap wasn't a physical event. I couldn't see it, or perceive it by any other sense, so how can I know the slap *was* wrong?

Roxana: Even to know that the slap occurred, you must have been able to recognize a slap when you saw one.

Sarah: Of course. When I see an event, I can classify it as a slap or not. I'm reliable enough, in good light.

Roxana: You saw an event and classified it as a misdeed. The light was good. Did you not recognize it as a misdeed?

Sarah: Well, I like to think I can recognize a misdeed when I see one. But I don't see how I *could* have developed any such capacity.

Roxana: What difference between slaps and misdeeds do you suppose relevant?

Sarah: Slaps look and sound similar to each other. Misdeeds don't.

Bob: I've seen and heard many slaps. They vary a lot: how hard and where the slap is given, who gives it, who gets it.

Zac: And a slap looks different from different points of view, Sarah.

Sarah: They still have a generic physical resemblance to each other. Misdeeds don't. Physical and mental abuse look and sound totally different.

Roxana: You can classify events without generic physical resemblance. Do you play chess?

Sarah: Sometimes. Why do you ask?

Roxana: You can recognize checkmate when you see it. Do all cases of checkmate have a generic physical resemblance?

Sarah: Not really. One checkmate often looks more similar to a situation that isn't checkmate than to another checkmate. The layout and number of pieces vary, even the pieces themselves. I've seen a chess set where they were cartoon characters. You're right, we can recognize much more abstract patterns in perception. But surely that's not enough for recognizing a misdeed when one sees it. Whether it's a misdeed depends on more background factors than whether it's checkmate. Someone committing bigamy can look exactly like them having a legitimate wedding.

Zac: What's wrong with bigamy between consenting adults, Sarah?

Sarah: The consent isn't usually informed. Anyway, I want to hear what Roxana says to my point.

Roxana: I will use a closer example. You can classify events as so-called misdeeds or not. By a 'so-called misdeed', I mean an event *you would call* a misdeed, whether or not it really is one.

Sarah: Of course. I classify them on the basis of similarity in my reactions. I feel moral disapproval, or I don't.

Roxana: No doubt.

Sarah: But the very question at issue is whether my feelings of moral disapproval or approval are warranted!

Roxana: That question comes later. For now, I do *not* assume that your feelings are warranted. I merely allow that you have them. My point should be uncontroversial. You respond differently to so-called misdeeds from other events. Your calling them misdeeds *is* one difference. So-called misdeeds already form a highly abstract pattern in the input to your brain, compared with slaps. Cases *you call* 'physical abuse' look and sound very different from cases *you call* 'mental abuse'. You can recognize so-called misdeeds. So it is stupid to say that misdeeds form too abstract a pattern for you to recognize them.

Sarah: But misdeeds are not the same as so-called misdeeds. I sometimes misclassify. When I'm misinformed about the background, I may mistake bigamy for a legitimate wedding, or a legitimate wedding for bigamy. Some so-called misdeeds are not misdeeds, and some misdeeds are not so-called misdeeds.

Roxana: Of course. I never said otherwise. You must listen more carefully. The point of my comparison was simply this: misdeeds and so-called misdeeds form patterns at a similar level of abstraction in the input to the brain. Since your brain is sensitive to the pattern formed by so-called misdeeds, do not tell me that the pattern formed by misdeeds is too abstract for your brain.

Sarah: I promise not to tell you that.

Roxana: That is satisfactory.

Sarah: I'm still worried about reliability. How could even a semi-reliable correlation be set up in the first place between what *I call* misdeeds and what *are* misdeeds?

Bob: Didn't your mum and dad teach you how to tell the difference between right and wrong?

Sarah: They certainly tried, but my morality is not exactly the same as theirs. Anyway, how did *they* know? If each generation passes the buck back to the previous one, how did it all get started?

Bob: I'd expect you to say it *evolved*.

Sarah: If we have it, it must have evolved somehow. But why would evolution favour morality? Evolution doesn't care about right and wrong, it only cares about fitness to survive and reproduce.

Bob: Does evolution care about anything?

Sarah: Of course not, strictly speaking. But how would the ability to distinguish right from wrong enhance our evolutionary fitness?

Bob: By helping us live together? If we keep murdering each other, we won't survive. How many animals kill others of the same kind? You must think that's evolution. Mind you, humans are worse than most.

Sarah: I see how a ban on murder could have evolved. But it evolved because murder tends to disfavour the survival of the species, not because murder is wrong. Perhaps murder is actually *right*, but we've evolved to think it wrong, and not do it. For all we know, the things we call 'misdeeds' are not misdeeds at all. We could have evolved to misidentify misdeeds.

Roxana: Do you also claim that, for all we know, the things we call 'slaps' are not slaps at all? Could we not have evolved to misidentify slaps?

Sarah: No, that would be absurd.

Roxana: What is the difference?

Sarah: I'm no general sceptic. I just worry about moral qualities, like rightness and wrongness, goodness and badness.

Roxana: Why are they so special?

Zac: Roxana, Sarah, wake up! The irreconcilable differences in morality between societies, between individuals, between epochs, show there are no moral qualities out there in the world, waiting for us to identify them, like botanists identifying plants.

Sarah: There are irreconcilable differences over science too. Bob will never give up his belief in witchcraft.

Bob: You will never give up your disbelief in it.

Sarah: The truth about witchcraft can be known. And the irreconcilable differences between scientists and religious fundamentalists about evolution don't stop scientists from knowing the truth of the evolutionary story. Something special about morality tempts me to be sceptical about it. I'm not sure how well I can explain it. We apply the words 'right' and 'wrong' in response to patterns in our environment, just as we use 'slap' and 'checkmate' and all sorts of other words. But 'right' and 'wrong' are special because we also use them to guide action. Calling an action 'right' gives it the green light: go. Calling it 'wrong' gives it the red light: stop.

Zac: That's what I said before, Sarah. Moral discourse guides action. It doesn't describe the world.

Sarah: No, it does both. That's the trouble. It risks a mismatch between the causes and effects of calling an action 'right' or 'wrong'.

Bob: What are you talking about, Sarah?

Sarah: I'll try an example. Some people think it's wrong to educate women. There's a real activity, educating women. They recognize it when they see it.

Bob: Anyone can see whether the pupils are boys or girls.

Sarah: But when the people I'm talking about see a girl being educated, it causes them to say 'That's wrong'. Then their judgement has an effect, people try to stop the education, since it's been given the red light. So there's a mismatch between the causes and effects of their judgement, since educating women shouldn't be stopped. How they apply moral terms sets up an inappropriate causal connection. My problem is, I can't see what's to stop a total mismatch between the causes and effects of moral judgements, ours just as much as theirs.

Roxana: That problem is not confined to moral discourse. It extends to all discourse about what to do.

Sarah: How do you mean?

Roxana: In solving any practical problem, people discuss what to do, even when no ethical issues arise. There may still be inappropriate connections between the causes and effects of their judgements of what to do.

Sarah: It would be silly to be sceptical about engineers' judgements of what to do when they are building a bridge, wouldn't it?

Roxana: How do you stop your scepticism generalizing to such cases?

Sarah: Let me think.... Perhaps the difference is this. The engineers are talking conditionally, about what to do *if you want the bridge not to fall down*. It's a matter of means to ends. Moral prohibitions aren't like that. They are meant to be unconditional, not just about means to ends. It's wrong for that woman to slap her son, even if she *wants* to hurt him. In fact, wanting to hurt him makes it even worse.

Bob: If I understand you correctly, Sarah, which I probably don't, how can you make such a neat separation between thinking about ordinary practical problems and thinking about right and wrong? It's no good me just thinking 'I must prune those roses if I want them to flourish'. I could think *that* even if I'd decided to get rid of them. I have to think 'I must prune those roses' full stop, no ifs or buts, otherwise I'll never get up off my backside, go out and actually prune them.

Sarah: You did understand me, Bob. I see what you mean. Someone who thought only things like '*If* this, then that' would be totally indecisive, even when it wasn't an ethical issue. To decide what to do, they have to get rid of the 'if'. Still, there's a difference between acting on practical grounds and acting on moral grounds.

Bob: How will you decide what to do if you keep the practical stuff in one compartment in your head and the moral stuff in another? You have to put them together. If those roses belong to someone else, who doesn't want them pruned, it's wrong for me to prune them, however much I want them to flourish and know they won't unless I do.

Sarah: You're right, when we're deciding what to do, we have to combine the practical considerations with the moral ones. If we keep them apart, one lot or the other will be sidelined once it's time to act.

Roxana: Then your moral thinking is an integral component of your whole system for making decisions?

Sarah: Yes, otherwise the moral thinking would be pointless.

Roxana: Does your scepticism apply just to the moral component, or to the whole system?

Sarah: What do you mean, sceptical about the whole system? It makes decisions, not predictions.

Roxana: In deciding what to do or not do, you reach a conclusion about what is or is not to be done. In deciding not to prune someone else's roses, Bob reached the conclusion that pruning the roses was not to be done. His conclusion was true if, and only if, pruning the roses *was* not to be done. It was false if, and only if, pruning the roses *was* to be done. I ask you whether you doubt Bob's conclusion or only the moral assumption on which he based it.

Sarah: Oh, I see. If the conclusion depends on the moral assumption, and I doubt the assumption, I'd better doubt the conclusion too. If a crucial component is dysfunctional, the system as a whole isn't going to work properly either. Since our moral values are a crucial component of our whole system for making decisions, if I'm sceptical about our moral values, I'd better be sceptical about our decision-making as a whole.

Bob: I'm getting lost again. How could moral values be dysfunctional?

Sarah: If your moral code forbids wearing clothes, it won't just lead you into morally questionable actions, it will mess up your life in practical ways too.

Bob: You'll freeze to death when winter comes.

Roxana: And is Sarah sceptical about our decision-making as a whole?

Sarah: That would be quite drastic, wouldn't it? People seem to get so many day to day decisions more or less right. Although they sometimes behave in self-destructive ways, more often than not they don't. Perhaps I shouldn't be so sceptical about our moral values after all.

Zac: Why is it crazy for a fallibilist like you to be sceptical of human decision-making as a whole, Sarah? Is our track record of success in action something to boast about, from your point of view?

Sarah: Certainly not. We make lots of mistakes in deciding what to do. That's obvious. But isn't it also obvious that we get lots of simple, everyday decisions more or less right?

Zac: 'Obvious'? Isn't that just us applauding ourselves, Sarah?

Sarah: It's better than that. No species could survive if its members usually messed up their decisions about what to do. Rats are pretty good at making practical decisions in their daily lives. Why should humans be so much worse?

Zac: Rats don't have to worry about morality, Sarah. They are beneath good and evil.

Sarah: Do you mean that morality obstructs good decision-making? It's a complication, no doubt. But doesn't evolution show that the effects of our moral values can't be too disastrous? Our species has survived, so we can't be too bad at decision-making, even with the burden of morality. We must be doing better than chance at avoiding false conclusions about what is to be done.

Zac: I'll grant you, Sarah, we are not much worse than rats at making decisions, from what you would call a purely practical point of view. But given where you are coming from, how can you exclude the possibility that our decisions are disastrously wrong according to the supposed 'true' morality? From your point of view, how do you know it doesn't tell our species to commit mass suicide?

Bob: If it does, I prefer immorality.

Sarah: Zac, you are assuming that I have two completely separate points of view, a purely practical one and a moral one. As Bob said, that won't work when I have to decide what to do. Then I integrate them into a single point of view. When I wanted a boat, morality said I couldn't steal one, practicality said I couldn't make one, so I had to buy one instead.

Bob: You could afford one.

Sarah: That was another practical consideration. Anyway, in deciding what is to be done, we mix moral considerations with purely practical ones. We assess other people's decisions, or our own past ones, in the same way. We judge whether the decision was correct or incorrect about what was to be done.

Zac: Sarah, isn't that just going through exactly the same decision-making process twice over and then saying it must be right?

Sarah: No. We have the benefit of hindsight. We judge decisions in retrospect by their results. That's an independent check.

Zac: We are still judging the results by the same moral values we used to make the decision in the first place, Sarah.

Sarah: Yes, unless we've changed our mind about them. Even if we haven't, that doesn't always mean that in hindsight we judge that we got the original decision right. The results sometimes show that we got it wrong. It's like science. We use science to interpret the results of our experiments, but that doesn't mean we never recognize that they have falsified our theory.

Zac: You like this analogy between science and decision-making, don't you, Sarah?

Sarah: Yes, I do. In science, you can be pretty confident that if a vital component of your total theory is hopelessly false, then the whole theory will make some false predictions. That works even if you can't test the faulty component in isolation. The same applies to our decision-making. And our moral values are a vital component of our decision-making.

Bob: You make it sound like a car.

Sarah: It is, in a way. Morality is like the brakes, not the CD player. It tells us *not* to do certain things, like murder, and it's not an optional extra.

Bob: I understand *that* comparison. But how can our decision-making be like science? Where are all the equations?

Sarah: We make decisions in a rough and ready way because everyday life is much messier and less controlled than scientific experiments, and everyday thinking is much less systematic and explicit than a scientific theory. But the same general principles apply. Of course, we already know that our decision-making involves many flaws and errors. One falsified prediction is no surprise.

Bob: What falsified prediction?

Sarah: Any clearly wrong decision, like deciding to burn witches.

Bob: Let's not go there again.

Sarah: Anyway, my analogy between decision-making and science still holds. We aren't completely incompetent at deciding what is to be done, which depends on our moral beliefs, so it's very improbable that they are hopelessly false.

Zac: Sarah, must I keep reminding you of all the irreconcilable differences over morality?

Sarah: No, Zac, you needn't. What those moral disagreements show is that most—probably all—societies and individuals have some—probably many—false moral beliefs. I don't dispute that. I'm only arguing against the scenario that worried me before, where our morality has no correlation with the truth at all. Moral disagreement amongst normal humans isn't anything like extreme enough to establish that scenario.

Roxana: There are irreconcilable differences over science too.

Zac: I have to say, Sarah, your talk of moral truth and your comparison of morality with science strike me as deeply inappropriate. Morality isn't just something cold and impersonal. It's about different ways of caring for other people.

Sarah: Such as burning them at the stake?

Bob: Sarah is a very caring person, Zac.

Sarah: Caring or not, I can be counter-suggestible. Zac inspires me to extend my analogy between morality and science. In the long run, science tends to correct its own errors. The same applies to morality. In the long run, it too tends to correct its own errors. So I'm optimistic: I look forward to moral progress as well as scientific progress.

Bob: Like what?

Sarah: We've learnt that slavery is wrong.

Roxana: For better or worse, Sarah has come a long way.

Bob: We all have. It's been a long journey.

Sarah: And after all this way, relativism has still got nowhere.

Zac: That's what you think, Sarah. From my point of view, it's kept going pretty nicely. Well folks, it's been a real pleasure getting to know you all, but I have urgent business further down the train before the journey ends. Roxana, I still hope one day to liberate you from the bondage of your logic.

Roxana: That is like offering to liberate me from the bondage of my skeleton.

Zac: Sarah, one day I hope you'll realize that science can't explain everything.

Sarah: Zac, one day science will explain why so many people *hope* it can't explain everything.

Zac: Bob, here's to your leg mending super-fast, and to a day when you and your neighbour see eye to eye.

Bob: If ever I lock gazes with a witch, it'll be the last thing I do.

Zac: I'd love to deconstruct your responses, but I must rush. *Au revoir*, Roxana, Sarah, Bob!

Sarah: Goodbye, Zac!

Bob: Bye.

Sarah: Poor Zac, he never gets it quite right, does he?

Roxana: He always gets it right from his own point of view.

Sarah: He was trying to get it right from our point of view too. That's where he failed.

Roxana: He got it right from our point of view, from his point of view.

Bob: What did he mean, 'deconstruct'?

Roxana: He meant that he would love to get his own back.

Sarah: Oh, look! He's talking to that woman in black.

Bob: The witch, you mean?

Sarah: That's her.

Bob: She *did* pick up one of his hairs as she passed. Does he look enchanted?

Sarah: He's talking animatedly. Does that count? Now they're looking into her bag, and laughing.

Bob: A bad sign.

Sarah: She looks enchanted.

Roxana: At last he has found a customer for his used car.

Sarah: I hope she won't pay too much for it.

Bob: When it breaks down she can always go back to the train.

Sarah: Amazingly, we even seem to be on time.

Roxana: No, we are one minute late.

Sarah: It's beginning to get dark.

Bob: The train is slowing down. We'll soon be at the station.

Sarah: Did you see that bird fly off from the tree? What was it?

Bob: It looked like an owl.

ACKNOWLEDGEMENTS

On this project my wife Ana Mladenović Williamson has been my most inspiring supporter and most unsparing critic. Many friends have contributed too: Ritchie Robertson, Katharine Nicholas, Jennifer Nagel, Amia Srinivasan, and Arno Waschk gave extensive detailed comments, and Ema Mimica, Marjanca Pakiž, Dušanka Nikolić, Miroslava Trajkovski, Dragan Trajkovski, Rae Langton, and Alex Tenenbaum useful reactions. For Oxford University Press, Peter Momtchiloff, Paul Boghossian, and two anonymous referees helped improve the book. Many thanks to all.